THE 256 ODÙ OF IFÁ

CUBAN AND TRADITIONAL

VOL. 4

Òjbè Òbàrà-Òjbè Òkànràn

MARCELO MADAN

NOTE TO THIS EDITION

As we have already noticed in our previous Ifá literatures, it is about transcription of manuscript documents, many of them unpublished, with different wording and literary styles, I have always tried to keep in essence, the idea of what was wanted to express, for Therefore, it is quite difficult to achieve uniformity of style in this regard. In this new presentation I show in each of the Odù, everything from the literature of **Afro-Cuban Ifá** and **African Traditional Ifá**.

It is in my interest, to provide Ifá students this time, a broad vision in all its dimensions of what Ifá can encompass, taking into account, in addition, that what is presented in this is not everything, because Ifá is much deeper. and his literary work is much more abundant than what I show here, this is only a part, even when I have added to these volumes' concepts from the previously published ifá treatises, as well as traditional ifá. In addition, it is not my intention here to suggest any kind of supremacy between the two trends, only to show them as each of them is presented and that it is the reader himself who judges and prefers its future use. My aim is to offer you the possibility of having at hand, a renewed tool for study, broader and more effective that allows you at the same time, to enter the learning of both literatures without limitations or discrimination, each one in its field, because ultimately, the knowledge of Ifá is universal and is for everyone alike.

iii

GRATEFULNESS

Thanks to Òlódùmarè, for having enlightened me and allow to create this work, to be able to throw the light of knowledge to everyone who needs it.

Thanks to Òrúnmìlà spirit of light that guides me and takes me along the right path.

Thanks to Òbàtála, my guard angel who always accompanies me and provides timely protection.

Thanks to my maternal grandmother and godmother Rosa Torrez (Ṣàngó Womí)

Thanks to my godfather Rubén Pineda Bàbá Éjìogbè

CONTENT

1- OGBÈ ÒBÀRÀ

+

I I
O I
O I
O I

I Pray:
Ogbè Bàrà bi Àboré bàbá àtelé A dífá fún sèsè, bi Àbo ré bàbá àtelé A dífá fún Şàngó, bi Àbo ré bàbá àtelé lodá fún Olófin. Bàbá Ọyèkún ko lade o oyé unlo awe re ni Òrúnmìlà to Iban Èşù.

IFA OF:
• Hidden Things
• Treason: where the Ministers told the king that he had to sacrifice his son to save the people and it was to destroy them.
• Maiden, talk about rape
• Phenomena

PROVERBS:
• The Jug that loses the bottom does not retain liquids.
• Edify the body. He is the owner of the rains
• The Bat with its head down, observes the way the birds

behave
- The ideas of a good man are like gold bars
- A King who dies, a King who eats. A dead King King put
- The white hen does not realize that she is an old bird.
- He who must play a role in life is recognized by his birth
- The big jar is never missing a hole
- The good sun is known at dawn
- If you dress naked and show your favor, you have not dressed him.
- The big jar cannot break itself.

BORN:
- The secret of breadfruit
- Let the birds feed their children by vomiting in their beaks.
- The linen fabric.
- Gesticulation when speaking.
- Why the head is prayed with white doves
- That the Ọṣẹ (soap) is removed in the Pinado forest of ọmọ Aganjù

(Pinado, Pinaldo, Pinardo, kuanaldo, etc: ceremony of consecration of the knife for the animal sacrifices that the Babalawos and Iworos receive)

BRAND
- Treason.
- Ear disease, don't neglect it, it can be serious.

SIGNALIZE
- In a patient who dies, because like the ewé Alukerese (the Hiedra), who lives attached to humidity, that person will live in humidity, in the grave.

- That in Itúto is favorable.
- That the person to achieve their wishes does not skimp on anything.
- Chest Disease.

IFÁ SAYS:
Of the family. There are sick
- The person is behind economically and everything
- Ṣàngó, you have to give Àgbò to Ṣàngó, to save him from Ikú
- To receive the Warriors, Òsányin and Ifá
- That ẹiyelé dies when squeezed in the chest
- Of the woman who can fail without getting married
- From an Eegún who speaks into your ear.
- That in this Ifá the godson goes out to find followers in religion and wants to be wiser than the godfather who consecrated him.
- That the person to achieve his wishes, does not skimp anything. Ifá of betrayal
- That the person has a secret in his life. Ifá of hidden things
- That here Ṣàngó was looking for a Jutía (Large Mountain Rat) to give to Elégbà, so that she would not interrupt him.
- That here the ministers told the King that he had to sacrifice his eldest son (first-born), to save his people and it was to destroy him as King and as man.
- Of decompositions, economic arrears and everything
- That bad things follow the Awo, as they followed Òrúnmìlà
- Bacán was born here, Ṣàngó was born whose father was called Ṣubulu Ado Madere Ayai Oku
- Of ear ailments, do not neglect that you can become deaf

3

- That here Olófin welcomes the person with open arms.
- That the godchildren of the Awo become enemies, as well as the person who is consulted.
- That Ògbè Bara is lost, if he thinks that he cannot live apart from the woman he loves
- That if the children do not do Ẹbọ, they will become enemies tomorrow
- That Ṣàngó is asked here, so that his destruction does not come
- You have to give the vulture food, because it represents the Awo Ògbè Bara
- That Olófin governs in this Ifá
- That in the Ituto ceremony, if Ògún leaves, Òṣósii also leaves, and if Ògún stays, Òṣósii also stays

PROHIBITIONS

- Trust nobody.
- Do not eat any large painted or red beans, they are served in front of your enemies
- Do not go to any gatherings or parties in painted clothing.
- Don't argue with anyone.

RECOMMENDATIONS

- If you have Olókun, change the jar.
- Wash the leri with breadfruit EWÉ leaves, Obí and egg white.
- Receive the Warriors, Òsányin and Ifá.
- Beware of lovers on the street.
- Take care of ear conditions.

- Beware of the door and the corners of your house that can hurt you.
- Be careful with parties and treats as there is betrayal in the environment.
- Be careful with alcoholic beverages because it can be your misfortune.
- Do not easily give your name to anyone without first finding out.
- If you are called, do not look back, if you do not recognize who it is. If he asks his name, tell him his name is Thin as a Needle.
- Give fresh meat to Ògún and Òşósii.
- Beware of lovers in the bus and on the street, because they can come to the house
- To progress, please feed Eegún on a rainy, stormy and lightning day

EWÉ ODÙ OGBÈ ÒBÀRÀ

Alukerese (Hiedra)—Avellanas-- Árbol del Pan

For more information see: Encyclopedia of Ifá herbs by Marcelo Madan

PATAKI LISTING
1. Ifá of the Traitor
2. The Disobedient Young Man (The three names of Şàngó)
3. Duality
4. Èşù Forún and the greatness of Ògbè Bara.
5. The War of the horse and the breadfruit
6. The Betrayal of the Dove
7. Here they wanted to sacrifice the king's son.

5

WORKS WITH OGBÈ ÒBÀRÀ

For Development
Elégbà is covered with mosquito netting at twelve o'clock, an Ìtanná is lit for him, three few drops of water are poured on the door and Agogó touches Ọbàtàlá asking for Health, tranquility and development.

Here the secret of the breadfruit leaf is born. When one is very confused, take two breadfruit leaves and an obi and wash the lerí in the form of a prayer and pour an egg white on it.
The lerí is also requested without fruit of the pair and egg white. It is also bathed with breadfruit leaves and egg white.
Work with Elégbà
He takes Elégbà and gets smeared with butter from eating, puts himself in the sun and when it is very hot, pour cold water on him and say to himself: Just as you have me, so I have you, you will give me what I want.

Work for development
Elégbà is covered with mosquito netting at 12 o'clock and is turned on and three drops of water are poured on the door and touched with agogo de Ọbàtàlá asking for owó.

Ẹbọ:
Àkúko fifeṣù, tiger leather, Àgbado grains, trap, three crowns, other ingredients, ọ pọ lọ pọ owó.
Ẹbọ: Ekuekueye (Ducks) méjì, 16 Ẹiyelé, palm heart, a white savanna, to do 2 lerí of igi (palo hueco), lizard, and gbogbo

6

tenuyen, other ingredients, ọ pọ̀ lọ̀ pọ̀ owó.
Iyere: Alaguana Fumi Lola Musoko

Take Elégbà and spread butter on it, put it in the sun and when it is very hot, pour cold water on it and say: That's how you have me, That's how I have you, you have to give me (you are asked what you want)
for stability
Take a cuje of igi rip belly, hang three güiritos, one painted red and loaded with eku, one white loaded with eja, and one painted black, loaded with àgbado and epo and leave it to Elégbà.

Work for Òbàtála
Òbàtála is given adié méjì funfun and 4 ẹiyelé funfun together with Osun, after cleaning all those present, all the jujú are removed from the adié and cooked well with orí and Òbàtála is given 16 days and is It is taken to the top of a hill, the adié are cooked well and Òbàtála is left for 3 days and one is taken to the riverbank and the other to the seashore.

Work with Elégbà
Take Elégbà and cover it with butter from eating, put it in the sun and when it is very hot, pour cold water on it and say: Just as you have me, so I have you, you will give me what I wanna.

Work for development
Elégbà is covered with mosquito netting at 12 noon and it is

7

turned on and three little drops of water are poured on the door and it is touched with agogo by Òbàtála asking him owó.

ẸBỌ:
Àkúko funfun méjì, Osaidie fifeşu, lerí de eja tútù méta, Àwòran méta, gbogbo ìleké, gbogbo aşọ, eko méta, atitan joro-joro, una okutá, eku, eja, epo, gbogbo ewé, opolopo owó.

ẸBỌ:
Àkúko méjì, beef bone, adié, a lerí of Àwòran, needles méta, aşọ ará, atitan Ilè, atitan bata, eku, eja, epo, àgbado, opolopo owó

ẸBỌ:
Àkúko fifeşù, tiger leather, àgbado grains, trap, three crowns, other ingredients, opolopo owó.

ẸBỌ:
Ekuekueye méjì, 16 ẹiyelé, palm kernel, a white sheet, 2 heads made of "palo hueco", chameleon, gbogbo Tenujen, other ingredients, opolopo owó.

Iyere: Alaguana Fumi Lola Musoko

ẸBỌ:
Òbúko, Àkúko méjì funfun, Paoyo, aşọ funfun, pupa, atitan

ilèkun, akarà, obí, efún, àgbado, malaguidí, eja, epo, opolopo owó.

<u>Èṣù Forun</u>

OGBÈ BARA PÀTAKI 1 IFA OF THE TRAITOR.

Pàtaki

Elégbà had a friend who was both one, but he betrayed him and went to take refuge in the land of ọfò. Elégbà, after much investigation, knew his whereabouts, took water, food and other necessary things for the road and left for the ọfò land, which was very distant, since Elégbà was in the Iyesá land with the firm idea of punishing and killing his enemy. .

Along the way Elégbà ran into two men who were on the same path, these men did not speak and walked without apparently knowing him, these two men were Ṣàngó and Òrúnmìlà and they did know where Elégbà was going, Òrúnmìlà so that Elégbà would not know him. Dressed in beggar's clothes, Elégbà wanted to eat and sat under a bush, just then Ṣàngó and Òrúnmìlà arrived and he offered them food and water, which they accepted with good wishes. Òrúnmìlà told Elégbà: Where you go you will no longer be able to do anything you think, because that person is dead, they finished eating and continued walking, they crossed at a crossroads which had two directions, Elégbà takes the one on the left and Ṣàngó and Òrúnmìlà the one on the right.

When Elégbà arrived in the land of Ọfò, he found out that

9

his enemy had already died and saying he already paid me, he left for his land, as soon as he arrived he met Ṣàngó and Òrúnmìlà where they made him know that they knew who he was, That is why we met you on the road to save you from not doing what you had planned, your enemy was punished by another who also betrayed, that is why between us there must always be great harmony, sympathy and this will be for life between us.

OGBÈ BARA PÀTAKI 2: THE DISOBEDIENT
YOUNG MAN (The three names of
Ṣàngó)
EBỌ: Àgbo, others ingredients, opolopo owó

Pàtaki

Once upon a time there was a young man who was very disobedient and he liked to go from town to town. On a certain occasion he came to a town and fell in love with a pretty girl and dishonored her, but at no time did she tell him her real name, she told him that her name was Kabiosile. He came to another town and did the same thing and told her his name was Ọba Kosó, some time passed and he came to another town and said his name was Ṣàngó, he also fell in love with a girl, on that occasion the girl's family reported him to the law, seeing that he was wanted by the justice system, he went to the house of Òrúnmìlà who saw this ifá and told him to do ẹbọ with Àgbo, the boy was quite disrespectful and left Òrúnmìlà waiting and he did not go, but things got worse and worse and returned to Òrúnmìlà's house, who told him: That he knew him with three different names and that from that moment he chose one, because he could not receive an inheritance that belonged to him, the young man paid attention to what Òrúnmìlà had told him and justice stopped persecuting him.

Of the three women he stayed with the most educated and he was happy because he did what Òrúnmìlà had indicated to him.

OGBÈ BARA PÀTAKI 3: THE DUALITY.

Pray:
Agba jigbo olewolaku kaka Erí méjì obírikiki baje fono karan ọmọ amanbi koşe mibi tanyi koditokobo kelebe ojwu kola geri Òdùdúwà Alawana Oní eti Egungun avala sewa apa mata opelerí mariwo Òrúnmìlà afuru bi oye adabidare Lodafún Eegún méjì ni Òdùdúwà.

ẸBỌ:
2 whistles, palm buds, 16 ẹiyelé, a white sheet, 2 bone stick heads, 1 chameleon, gbogbo Tenujen, $Money

Pàtaki

Òdùdúwà Alawana was a very powerful being, who had a very large brain that would allow him to live in the world around him while he lived in the inner world of the spirit, with which he could live two lives at the same time, but sometimes when he was with all his power for the inner world, he did not hear what his children told him and they believed he was deaf, his children were Aguema.

11

One day Òrúnmìlà went home, and seeing his state made Osode for him and this ifá came out, where he made ẹbọ with two whistles and when he blew Òdùdúwà Alawana woke up from the inner world to his material world, coming down from his house that It was the palm, to the earth covered with a white sheet, fulfilling everything that his children requested, rendering Moforibale to Òrúnmìlà, because thanks to him Òdùdúwà Alawana, through Ogbè Bara, was able to communicate with the two worlds, material and spiritual.

Note:

The secret of Alawana is called Kara Eru Awó, they are two heads that are carved in bone stick, loaded with palm root, ero, obí kola. Osun, obí motiwao, lerí ẹiyelé, Eegún, Aguema, these heads eat ẹiyelé with Òdùdúwà, two whistles go on them, one open and the other closed, they are covered with a white cloth and the Eegún of the load are Mokékéré and Arugbo, yes were Albinos better.

OGBÈ BARA PÀTAKI 4 ÈṢÙ FORUN IS THE GREATNESS OF OGBÈ BARA.

Pray:

Ogbè Bara ikiyo Lodafún orika mogun oda onile Ògún lorubo Àkúko lebo bate aya Èṣù eta mota Àkúko ekú, eja.

Pray:

Elebo Èṣù Forun Òrúnmìlà unlo Ilè Ifé Inlé Ògún Lodafún Elégbàra ṣonṣon ado.

ẸBỌ:

12

Àkúko, ekú, eja, inṣu, Aya, maníes méta.

Pàtaki

Òrúnmìlà, who in that land was called Ogbè Bara, had come from very far and arrived at Ifé, which was ruled by Ògún and Elégbà. Ogbè Bara began to divine in that land where he acquired fame, having many godchildren and money, but his greatest aspiration was to become Ọba of that land. But in his eagerness, he forgot that he had to count first with the kings of that land who were Òrùn, Elégbà and Ògún.

Elégbà had a baby Àkúko in his yard and he was pleased to see them, but one day Ogbè Bara ordered ẹbọ to be done with one of Elégbà's Àkúko and when he found out, he rebuked him in front of Òrùn and Ògún accusing him of using alien animals in his ẹbọses , then Òrùn and Ògún threw Ogbè Bara out of the land of Ifé and he had to go on a pilgrimage through the land of the Òrìṣà where he met a very strange character who rode an Òbúko that character was Èṣù Forun and he told him if you You feed me, I give you my help to get up, but you have to be humble and forget about your desire to command, because you were born to order things, but you cannot have command in the land of Ifé, only in the land of the Òrìṣà, only with my help you will achieve the respect of your peers Ogbè Bara told him, it's fine, and he took Èṣù Forun and gave him food that he asked for, and in this way he managed to dominate the land of the Òrìṣà, and from Ifé they watched as Ogbè Bara ruled the land of the Òrìṣà. And then they started calling him

13

again. That, although he had no command in the land of Ifé, he became necessary and appointed thanks to Èṣù Forun and Òrúnmàle Òrìṣa.

OGBÈ BARA PÀTAKI 5: THE WAR OF THE HORSE AND THE BREADFRUIT

ẸBỌ: Àkúko méta, Euré dudu, a mat, an underwear

Pàtaki

Temu was the most famous Awó that the land of Obí Aya Nile had and Olókun who lived in that land was always complaining and tearful because his wife had never had a child and so he decided to consult with Awó Temu to see what he said, Awó Temu This Ifá saw him, that he had to do ẹbọ so that his wife would give birth, he also told him that even if he did not do ẹbọ, his wife would give birth, but that the ẹbọ should do it so that the children would not have enemies later, Olókun performed the ẹbọ but he left it incomplete because he did not bring the Àkúko méta that he was wearing when his wife gave birth, it turned out that he brought Jimaguas and named him Eṣin and Afon, which means the Horse and the other the Breadfruit Tree.

The years passed and his descendants had the same thing happen to their father Olókun, they wanted to have descendants and they went to the house of Awó Temu who marked him ẹbọ that years ago he had marked his father and the same thing happened again they did not bring the three

Àkúko who carried the ẹbọ and this was incomplete during Eṣin's pregnancy, Afon's wife had a son Eṣin wondered what was happening that his wife did not finish giving birth and went to Temu's house and Temu told him that the ẹbọ he had brought his brother for him was not complete since the three Àkúko were missing, so Eṣin got angry and went to Afon's house and began to trample on Afon's children until he killed them. Then, as time passed, Eṣin's wife gave birth to a boy and when Afon found out, she brought him water and she gave him so much that she drowned him. Since then Eṣin and Afon are deadly enemies. Along this path you have to do the complete ẹbọ

OGBÈ BARA PÀTAKI 6: THE BETRAYAL OF LA PALOMA

Pàtaki

At the beginning of the world all the Birds tried to kill the Dove. And they prepared a trap with glue, in order to catch her alive, the pretext was that they were going to throw a big party in her name. But the Dove before going she went to Òrúnmìlà's house and made ẹbọ and later she attended the banquet. She perched on a tree and when they went to get hold of her, she took flight. Thus, discovering the betrayal that was plotted against her.

OGBÈ BARA PÀTAKI 7: THIS IS WHERE THEY WANTED TO SACRIFICE THE KING'S SON.

Pàtaki

Once the Bábàlawós advised the king that, in order to save himself and his people, he had to sacrifice his son, and they gave so much that the king consented. When the date of the sacrifice approached, everyone went to see and among the procession that arrived at the place was Òrúnmìlà, who heard that a prisoner sang. And he wondered how, being the son of a king, they were going to slaughter him? Then Òrúnmìlà ordered the prisoner to be brought to him and he told him what happened. Immediately Òrúnmìlà went to see the king and asked him: ¿What happened to you? And he replies that the Bábàlawós advised him to sacrifice his firstborn. But this is Àgbo, not his son, answered Òrúnmìlà. Then Òrúnmìlà called the Bábàlawós and they all had to agree that the firstborn was Àgbo, not the king's son. Where they released the king's son and sacrificed Àgbo.

Note:

Whoever gets this letter has to give a ram to Şàngó to save him from death.

2- TRADITIONAL IFÀ ÒGBÈ ÒBÀRÀ

ÒGBÈ ÒBÀRÀ VERSE 1

Ogbè gbàràdá tán;

Tẹlẹgàn ló kù;

Ifá ṣeun gbogbo tán;

Ò ku tẹlẹnu;

Díá fún Ẹ̀dú;

Ọmọ agbápà lápà;

Ọmọ agbé rekete lóríi rekete

Translation:
Ogbè had performed wonders

Only critics are not satisfied

Ifá had successfully achieved all things

Only calumnies remain

These were the declarations of Ifá to Èdú (Òrúnmìlà)
He who increases wonders upon wonders
And he piles wonderful things on top of other wonderful things

PROPHESY
Ifá says that it predicts the Iré of prosperity for you to whom Ogbè-Gbarada is revealed. Ifá says that you will have abundant prosperity and your success will multiply despite the slander. Ifá says that you will have a very important personality in society.

Pataki

Òrúnmìlà had been doing many wonderful things on Earth. At the same time, he had many slanders, critics and slanderers who did not want him to succeed. Therefore, he went to consult the students of his mentioned above. They advised him to offer sacrifices of two hens and money. He complied.

Soon after, he became very successful and all his followers also became very successful. His popularity spread and widened. So, they became happy, singing and dancing:
Ogbè had performed wonders
Only the critics are not satisfied
Ifá had successfully achieved all things
Only calumnies remain
These were the declarations of Ifá to Èdú (Òrúnmìlà)
He who increases wonders upon wonders
And he piles wonderful things on top of other wonderful

things
The wonders performed by Ifá
They can't be snatched
They just keep multiplying
The wonders that Ifá has authorized me to perform
They can never be destroyed

Ifá says that no one can stop the person for whom this Odù is released from being successful in his life.

ÒGBÈ ÒBÀRÀ VERSE 2

Òpìpì yéyin níwọn;

Kóo lè baà r'ápá bẹyin;

Díá fún pẹhẹẹ;

Ọmọ af'adìẹ ṣèpilẹ ọlà

Translation
(Òpìpì) hen without feathers

Don't lay too many eggs

So, your wings can cover all your eggs

This was Ifá's declaration to PẸ̀HẸ́Ẹ́

The result of who arranged the foundation of this success with a chicken.

PROPHESY

Ifá says that it also predicts an Iré of abundance (wealth) for you. Ifá says that you need to offer the appropriate sacrifice in order to accelerate the realization of this abundance.

Pataki

Pẹhẹẹ wanted to start a business. Therefore, he contacted the Babaláwo mentioned above for an Ifá consultation. He was advised to offer sacrifice with two hens without wings. The Babaláwo assured him that he would be successful in his business venture. He complied.

The Babaláwo made the sacrifice for him and returned the chickens to him so that he could raise them in his house. Most of the hens laid eggs that hatched, the most successful Pẹhẹẹ came to him. He was very happy and gave blessings to his Babaláwo for a job well done:

Òpìpì yéyin níwọn;

Kóo lè baà r'ápá b'ẹyin;

Díá fún Pẹhẹẹ;

Ọmọ af'adìẹ ṣè'pìlẹ ọlà;

Kòì pẹ, kòì jìnnà;

Káwá bá ni nì jẹbútú ajé gburugburu

Translation:
(Òpìpì) hen without feathers

Don't lay too many eggs

So, your wings can cover all your eggs

This was Ifá's statement to Pẹhẹẹ

The result of who arranged the foundation of this success

with a chicken

Before long, not too long

He found us in the midst of abundant wealth

People are in the midst of abundant wealth at the foot

of the sacred palm

Ifá says that you will be a millionaire and very successful in

life.

ÒGBÈ ÒBÀRÀ VERSE 3

Bààrà-baara làá g'étì;

Sónsó oríi rè loògùn;

Sónsó oríi rè làwúre;

Díá fún Òrúnmìlà;

Baba yóó kúnlè sorò jeun tuntun lódún;

Ò wá ndánu sùnráhùn Ire gbogbo

Translation:
Abundantly, we deposit ETÌ
Only the top of his head is medicine
Only the top of his head is used for medicine for success in finances
These were the declarations of Ifá to Òrúnmìlà
When she was preparing for the new harvest of the festival
And she was wanting all the IRE in life

PROPHESY
Ifá says that he also predicts an Iré of abundance (wealth) for you. Ifá says that in addition to being a millionaire, you will also be able to participate in successful adventures.

Pataki
The new harvest of the festival was drawing near. Òrúnmìlà was preparing for this festival, but he had no money. He had no farm from which to get produce and no pond from which to harvest fish. As a result of this, Òrúnmìlà approached his students mentioned above for an Ifá consultation. What was he going to do to succeed before the day of the festival? How was he going to get the money to avoid being disgraced during the festival period? Being a holder of a title and a very popular person in the community, Òrúnmìlà considered it a great cause for concern not to participate fully in the festival physically, normally, administratively and financially.
The Babaláwo advised him to offer a sacrifice and they assured him that everything would be fine. Òrúnmìlà was asked to offer two hundred sacrificial snails. He was also asked to pack a suitcase with white clothes. He complied. He gave the two hundred snails to the Babaláwo who mixed

them turning them with ÌYẸRÒSÙN and recited this stanza within him. Both the snails and ÌYẸRÒSÙN were then packed inside the suitcase and he returned it to Òrúnmìlà. They asked him to do their business with the money and they also put all his money inside the suitcase. He too complied with this advice and followed the instructions.

Before the day of the festival, his spirit guides attracted many clients and business associates to him. All his projects and investments were very successful. Òrúnmìlà was very happy and was giving blessings to his Babaláwo.

Bààrà-baara làá g'étì;

Ṣónṣó oríi rẹ loògùn;

Ṣónṣó oríi rẹ làwúre;

Díá fún Òrúnmìlà;

Baba yóó kúnlẹ ṣorò jẹun tuntun lọdún;

Ò wá ndánu sùnráhùn Ire gbogbo;

Wọn ní kó rúbo;

Ò rúbo;

Kòì pẹ, kòì jìnnà;

Ẹ wá bá ni ní jẹbútú Ire gbogbo

Translation:
Abundantly, we deposit ẸTÌ
Only the top of his head is medicine
Only the top of your head is needed for medicine for

23

financial success.

They were the ones who launched Ifá for Òrúnmìlà

When he was preparing for the new harvest of the festival

And I was wanting all the IRE in life

He was advised to offer sacrifice

he fulfilled

Before long, not too long

Come join us in the midst of abundant IRE

Ifá says that the person for whom this Odù is revealed is currently entertaining himself with some fears about the proper functioning of his finances. You have no reason to fear. Everything would turn positive for you.

ÒGBÈ ÒBÀRÀ VERSE 4

Bààrà-baara làá g'ẹtì;

Şónşó oríi rẹ loògùn;

şónşó oríi rẹ legbòogi;

Díá fún 'Fátóóyangàn;

Tíí şọmọ bíbí inú Àgbonìrègún

Translation:

Abundantly, we deposit ẸTÌ

Only the top of his head is medicine

Only the top of his head is grass

They were the ones who launched Ifá for Ifátóóyangàn

24

The child of Àgbonìrègún

PROPHESY

Ifá says that he will assure you of success. Ifá says that, if it is during the ÌKỌSÈDÁYÉ of a newborn baby, the name of the child or baby is IFÁTÓÓYANGÀN. Whoever this Odù is revealed to, will have to undergo the ÌTẸLÓDÙ ceremony.

Pataki

Ifátóóyangàn (Ifá deserves to be proud of being one) was the child of Àgbonìrègún. He had everything in life through Ifá. He had money, land properties, farms, houses, children, happiness and all the good things in life through Ifá. He was always feeling proud of his achievements. Those who were sent from his successes and achievements were told, however, to go and study Ifá if they wanted the same things.

Bààrà-baara làá g'ẹtì;

Şónşó oríi rẹ loògùn;

Sónşó oríi rè legbòogi;

Díá fún Ifátóóyangàn; T

íí şọmọ bíbí inú Àgbọnìrègún;

Ifá tóó yangàn fọmọ Awo;

Ẹni tó pé Ifá ò tóó yangàn;

Kó lọ rèé kọ'fá;

25

Ifá tóó yangàn fọmọ Awo

Translation:

Abundantly, we deposit ẸTÌ
Only the top of his head is medicine

Only the top of his head is grass

They launched Ifá for Ifátóóyangàn

The child of Àgbonìrègún

Ifá is worthy of being proud of the Awo

Anyone who says that Ifá is not worthy of being proud

Let it go and study Ifá

Ifá is worthy of being proud of the Awo

Ifá says that the client will have reason to be proud of the achievements that he has had through Ifá. Whatever achievements are sent to you, you should also be advised to take the path of Ifá. You should, however, endeavor to undergo the ÌTÈLÓDÙ ceremony as soon as possible.

ÒGBÈ ÒBÀRÀ VERSE 5

Ogbè bàràrà-baara g'ẹtì;
Ṣónṣó oríi rẹ loògun;

26

Şónşó oríi rẹ legbòogi;

Díá fún Erin;

Ó n lọ gun Òkè-Àlọ baba rẹ

Translation:

Abundantly, we deposit ẹtì

Only the top of his head is medicine

Only the top of his head is grass

They were the ones who launched Ifa for Elephant

When he was going to his father's mountain of success

PROPHESY
Ifá says that Ifá will perform wonders in the life of his client.
The client's movements and the transformation thanks to
the herbs will be so fast that it will leave many people in awe.
It would be so fast that many people would find it hard to
believe.

Pataki
In ancient times, the Elephant was as big as a rat. There were
so many things that the Elephant planned to do, which his
diminutive size could not allow him to carry out.
Consequently, he went to the Babaláwo mentioned above
for an Ifá consultation.
The Babaláwo assured the Elephant that he would become
a great person in life. He was advised to offer sacrifice of

four new mortar shells, four guinea fowl, four hens and abundant money. He complied. Then the Babaláwo prepared some spiritual medicines for the Elephant. While the Babaláwo did this to him, the Elephant was asked to put each of his limbs inside each mortar. In no time, his limbs became as big as the size of four mortars and his trunk became as big as a small mountain. The mortars became the feet of the Elephant.

Those who saw the Elephant when he entered the Babaláwo's house could not recognize him when he left. When other animals eventually realized that the Elephant had become very large, they all respected, revered and feared him. They were also in awe of how he managed to get so big.

Ogbè bààrà-baara làá g'ẹtì;

Şónşó oríi rè loògùn;

Şónşó oríi rẹ legbòogi;

Díá fún Erin;

Ò n lọ gun Òkè-Àlọ baba rẹ;

Wéré la r'Érin;

Érin nígbàwo lo g'òkè

Translation:

Abundantly, we deposit Ẹtì

Only the top of his head is medicine

28

Only the top of his head is grass

They were the ones who launched Ifa for Elephant

When he was going to his father's mountain of success

Suddenly we saw the Elephant

Elephant, when did you achieve this dimension?

Ifá says that you will become very important in the community.

ÒGBÈ ÒBÀRÀ VERSE 6

Tọpọ tẹri;

Díá fún Ẹṣin;

A bù fún Àfọn;

Wọn ní kí àwọn méjèèjì bọ'rí ara wọn

Translation:

Tọpọ-tẹri

He was the one who launched Ifá for the Horse

He threw the same for the fleshy African fruit

They were advised to perform a ritual to the Orí of each

PROPHESY

Ifá says that it is advisable for you and one of your relatives (born of the same mother), to offer sacrifice so that the Orí of one would support that of the other. They must perform the ritual to their Orí. In other words, you will buy all the materials for the Orí of your relative, while your relative will also reciprocate in the same way.

Pataki

Both Horse and Fleshy Fruit were partners. They both went with the Babaláwo mentioned above to investigate from Ifá what they both needed to do to succeed in life. The Babaláwo advised them to offer a sacrifice of two Guinea fowl each and money. They were also advised to perform the ritual for the Orí on each other as explained above. They were also asked to confirm from Ifá the necessary materials to use in their Orí. They complied.

From that day, when one was depressed, the Ori of the other would assist him and the one who was depressed would get up again. They both succeeded and were happy in their lives.

Tọpọ tẹri;

Díá fún Ẹṣin;

A bù fún Àfọn;

Wọn ní kí àwọn méjèèjì b'Ọrí araa wọn;

Wọn gbẹbọ wọn rúbọ;

Kàkà k'Áwo má là o;

30

Àfọn a tara kàrà a so

Translation
Tọpọ Tẹri

He was the one who launched Ifá for the Horse

He threw the same for the African Fleshy Fruit

They were advised to perform the Orí ritual from one to

another

they fulfilled

In the place of the Horse did not triumph

African Fleshy Fruit would germinate quickly

In the place of the Awo, he did not triumph

African fleshy fruit would grow rapidly

Ifá says that the two companions of Orí will support each

other to succeed. So, when one gets down, the other will

pick him up.

ÒGBÈ ÒBÀRÀ VERSE 7

Obìnrin rọṣọ tán;

Ó ṣe ìdí ṣàngelè sẹyìn;

Díá fún Nọmu;

Ó n fomi ojú sùngbérèe tọmọ;

31

Wọn ní kó sákáalẹ ẹbọ ní ṣíṣe;

Ó gbẹbọ, ó rúbọ

Translation:

A woman knotted her wrap

And she threw back some buttocks in a suggestive way

She was the only one who launched Ifá for Nọmu

When she was crying because she couldn't give birth to a baby

She was advised to offer sacrifice

she fulfilled

PROPHESY

Ifá says that she predicts an Iré of many children for you. Ifá says that the woman in question, she will father so many children that she will be the envy of her colleagues. Many other women will be praying to the gods to bless them with as many children as you. A stanza in Ogbè 'Gbàràdá giving evidence of her statement says:

Pataki

Nọmu married as a teenager. But unfortunately, she was not able to give birth to a child. Consequently, she went to Ifá for a consultation. She was assured that she would father many children. She was advised to offer sacrifice with two hens, two pigeons and money. They also asked him to perform a ritual of two rats, two fish, four kola nuts, four bitter kola, gin and money to Ifá. She complied.

Shortly after, her uterus opened and she gave birth to many children. Most of her acquaintances were praying to the gods to give them many children like Nomu.

Obìnrin rọ̀ṣọ́ tán;

Ó sèdí ṣàngèlè sẹ̀yìn;

Díá fún Nọmu;

Ó n fomi ojú sùngbérèe tọmọ;

Wọn ní kó sákáalẹ̀ ẹbọ ní ṣíṣe;

Ó gbẹbọ, ó rúbọ; Kò pẹ́, kò jìnnà;

Ire ọmọ wá ya dé tùrtúru;

Èmi á bímọ bíi Nọmu;

Èmi á bí Qwènnèwẹnnẹ lọmọ

Translation:

A woman knotted her wrap

And she threw back some buttocks in a suggestive way

She was the only one who launched Ifá for Nọmu

When she was crying because she couldn't give birth to a baby

She was advised to offer sacrifice

she fulfilled

In a short time, not too long

The IRE of many children came in droves

I will give birth to as many children as Nomu

I will beget children abundantly

Ifá says that she predicts an Iré of many healthy children for you.

ÒGBÈ ÒBÀRÀ VERSE 8

Kòkò Òdù, ab'enu kùndún-kùndun;

Díá fún Ojú-mọ-rìíbi;

Tíí şe Àrẹmọ Ọsányìn;

Wón ní kó sákáalẹ ẹbọ ní şíşe o;

Ó gbẹ'bọ, ó rúbo

Translation:
The giant jar with a narrow mouth

He was the one who launched Ifá for "Don't-let-my-eyes-see-the-demon" (Ojú-mo-rìíbi)

Who was the first son of Òsányìn

He was advised to offer sacrifice

he fulfilled

PROPHESY

Ifá says that he will not allow you to see the demon in his dream. Ifá says that no matter the situation in life, you will not even remotely experience the witness of the devil as it happens to those (who are close to you) and whose problems could affect you in adversity.

Pataki

Ojúmorìíbi was the first son of Òsányìn, the Deity of Medicine. Ojúmorìíbi went to the Babaláwo mentioned above to find out what he needed to do in order to prevent his two eyes from witnessing the demon or experiencing calamity in his life. The Babaláwo told him that Ifá had assured him that he would never experience calamity in his life. He was advised to make sacrifice of a he-goat and money. He was also advised to perform a ritual with a rooster, palm oil and money to Òsányìn. He complied. Later, the Babaláwo buried the native chalk (Efun), sawdust (Osun), the Seashell (Ìwónrán Olókun) and Eyìn-Olobe went together, recited this stanza at the same time and gave it to Ojú-mo-rìíbi so that drink with gelatinous porridge or water. He also complied with that.

Throughout the life of Ojú-mo-rìíbi he never experienced

35

calamity nor did he witness seeing the demon that could affect him with adversity by proxy. Therefore, he lived a very happy and contented life until his death.

Kòkò Òdù, ab'enu kùndún-kùndun;

Díá fún Ojú-mọ-rìíbi;

Tíí se Àrẹmọ Ọ̀sányìn;

Wón ní kó sákáalẹ ẹbọ ní şíşe;

Ó gbẹ'bọ, ó rúbo;

Ifá ló ní ojúù mi ò nìí ríbi lóde ìsálayé;

Ojú ẹfun kìí ríbi lóde Òsogbo;

Ojú osùn kìí ríbi lóde Ìràwọ;

Ojú iwọnrán kìí ríbi ló'Kun;

Léyìn- léyìn l'olobe nsoó sí

Translation:

The giant jar with a narrow mouth
He was the one who launched Ifá for "Do-not-let-my-eyes-see-the-demon" (Ojú-mọ-rìíbi)
Who was the first son of Ọ̀sányìn
He was advised to offer sacrifice
he fulfilled
Ifá has ordered that my eyes will not see evil in this world
The eyes of Efun (native chalk) see no evil in the village of

Òsogbo

The eyes of Òsùn (sawdust) do not see evil in the town of Ìràwọ

The eyes of Ìràwọ (seashell) do not see evil within the sea

Olobe's departure always pays off on his return

(evil would always happen upon my return)

Ifá says that you would have left the neighborhood, before the disaster started. However, you could not fall into a legal calamity or disaster, because Ifá has assured you.

ÒGBÈ ÒBÀRÀ VERSE 9

BàÀrà-baara làá g'ẹtì;

Şónşọ oríi rẹ loògùn;

Şónşọ oríi rẹ l'egbòogi;

Díá fún Àrágberí;

Omo akàn'lèkùn ọrun gbọngbọn má yùn-ún

Translation:

Abundantly, we deposit ẹtì

Only the top of his head is medicine

Only the top of his head is grass

They were the ones who launched Ifá for Àrágberí

Who knocked loudly on heaven's door, but refused to enter

PROPHESY

Ifá says that the client for whom this Odù is revealed still has a very serious illness, or had a close relationship with whom he has a very serious illness. Ifá says that the sick person will overcome this disease, if the appropriate sacrifice is made. Even though this disease is almost hopeless, the person will survive. What you need to do is offer sacrifice, perform a ritual to Ifá and its celestial double (Ègbè).

Pataki

Àrágberí was very ill. He had nightmares about the daily basics. He also had visions of his dead ancestors in his dreams. Many of his relationships had given up hope of survival. But even with all these setbacks, Àrágberí himself trusted that he would survive the disease. Therefore, he went to the house of the Babaláwo mentioned above for an Ifa consultation.

The Babaláwo who launched Ifá for Àrágberí and Ogbè-Gbàràdá was revealed. The Babaláwo told him that during his heavenly visit (Ẹgbẹ) they were preparing a great reception for him in heaven and that they were eagerly awaiting his arrival. The Babaláwo said that Àrágberí needed to offer, with an urgent stamp, a sacrifice of two rams, palm oil and money. One of the two rams should be offered as a sacrifice while the other ram would be used to perform an Ifá ritual. The sacrificial one would first be ridden by the sick person for some time before being sacrificed. Àrágberí was also required to offer akara, ekọ, moinmoin, assorted food and drink to his Ẹgbẹ. He complied. The reason why

38

Àrágberí should mount the ram before offering it in sacrifice was to give the heavenly visitor and Death the impression that Àrágberí was riding the ram towards heaven. But since it is impossible for the ram to support the weight of a mature person, then the ram could not move. Consequently, it was not Àrágberí who refused to heed Death's call and his heavenly visit, but the ram had refused to take him to heaven.

This was done several times, but the ram could not walk. This ram was eventually offered as a sacrifice while the remains of the sacrificial material were also offered. Èsù Odara then went to convince Death and the heavenly visits of Àrágberí that Àrágberí's refusal to come to heaven was not his attitude but that of the ram that had refused to take him to heaven. Since the ram had been offered as a sacrifice, it was advisable to take it to heaven instead of Àrágberí. They accepted the ram and left Àrágberí alone. Since then, Àrágberí became healthy and was very happy afterwards. He was giving his gratitude to the Babaláwo while the Babaláwo was praising Ọrúnmìlà and he thanked praising Olódùmarè.

Bàànà-baara làá g'ẹtì;

Ṣónṣọ orí rẹ loògùn;

Ṣónṣọ orí rẹ l'egbòogi;

Díá fún Àrágberí;

Omo akàn'lèkùn ọrun gbọngbọn má yùn-ún;

Ògúnlénírún agogo;

Ọ̀tàlégbèje àpèsìn;

Ni wọn fi n p' Àrágberí lọrun; Ẹbọ ló fi n şọwọ sí wọn;

Ẹbọ ló fi n ti ilẹ̀kùn ọrun gbọngbọn;

Ogúnlénírún agogo;

Ọ̀tàlégbèje àpèsìn;

Ni wọn fi n pé Àrágberí lọrun kó jẹ o;

Ẹ bá mí wi fún wọn;

Wípé ònà ọrun jìn gbungbun;

Àgbò Ẹ̀dú mà kọ'rìn.

Translation:

Abundantly, we deposit ẹtì

Only the top of his head is medicine

Only the top of his head is grass

They were the ones who launched Ifá for Àrágberí

Who knocked loudly on heaven's door, but refused to enter

Four hundred and twenty musical bells

One thousand four hundred and sixty drums

They were being used to summon Àrágberí to heaven

It was a sacrifice that he was sending back to heaven

It was rituals that he was using to close the gate of heaven firmly.

Four hundred and twenty musical drums

One thousand four hundred and sixty drums

They were being used to summon Àrágberí to heaven, but he refused to go

Help me inform them (in heaven)

That the road to heaven is very far

Edu's ram refused to move

Ifá says that the client will overcome his illness no matter how serious this illness is.

ÒGBÈ ÒBÀRÀ VERSE 10

Ogbè níí bo Àrìrà molè;

Àrìrà níí bolè;

Níí bogi oko;

Díá fún Olúkòso-làlú;

Jènrolá, omo arígba-ota şegun;

Igbà ti nbè láàrin otá

Translation:

Ogbè is the one that covers the thunder of the storm

Lightning is the one that covers the earth

And covers the trees on the farm

They were the ones who launched Ifá for Olúkòso-làlú

Jẹnrọlá, the one who used 200 pebbles to defeat opponents

When he was in the midst of enemies

PROPHESY
Ifá predicts an Iré of victory over his adversary. Ifá says that you need to offer sacrifice and perform rituals to Shàngó.

Pataki

Ṣàngó was sleeping and getting up in the midst of his enemies. It was difficult for him to make any decision in his life. Tired of his existence, Ṣàngó went for an Ifá consultation. How could he defeat his enemies?

The Babaláwo assured him that he would be feared, respected and revered by his enemies. Both friend and foe would not be able to meet him forcefully. Ṣàngó was then advised to offer in sacrifice a rooster, palm oil and 200 pebbles with a large mortar and money. He complied. The mortar was placed down on the shore with the 200 pebbles inside and the ritual was performed to Ṣàngó with another rooster. While the enemies were plotting against the demon, the thunder from the sky and all the enemies of him

42

scattered "HELTER-SKELETER". Even Ṣàngó's friends felt his power and controlled themselves with fear. In this way it was possible for Ṣàngó to defeat all his enemies and from that day on he was feared and respected by both friends and enemies.

Ogbè níí bo Àrìrà mọlẹ;

Àrìrà níí bo lẹ;

Níí bogi oko;

Díá fún Olúkòso-làlú;

Jẹnrọlá, ọmọ arígba-ota ṣẹgun;

Igbà ti nbẹ láàrin ọtá;

Wọn ní kó sákáalẹ, ẹbọ ní ṣíṣe;

Ò gbẹbọ, ó rụbọ;

Èdọọ yín ì bá gbó;

Ẹ ó dúró d'Àrìrà;

Kí l'Àrìrà fi sẹtẹ?;

Igba ọta; L'Àrìrà fi ṣẹtẹ;

Igba ọta

Translation:

Ogbè is the one that covers the thunder of the storm
Lightning is the one that covers the earth

43

And covers the trees on the farm

They were the ones who launched Ifá for Olúkòso-làlú

Jẹnrọlá, the one who used 200 pebbles to defeat opponents

When he was in the midst of enemies

He was asked to offer sacrifice

he he fulfilled

If your liver is as strong as you think (if you are as bold as you think)

Why can't you wait and confront the Lightning

What was it that the Ray used to defeat the conspiracy

two hundred pebbles

What was it that Ṣàngó used to defeat the conspiracy

two hundred pebbles

Ifá says that you will defeat your enemies and their conspiracies. Both friend and foe will fear and respect him.

ÒGBÈ ÒBÀRÀ VERSE 11

Òkú ló kú;

Ará ọrun ò sunkún;

A bímọ láyé;

À nyò sẹsẹẹsẹ;

Ọ́sán lòru ẹbọra eni;

Díá fún Alákọlé;

Ọmọ atìkùn sájà fara yíyí a dífá;

Wón ni kó sákáalẹ, ẹbọ ní ṣíṣe;

Ó gbẹ́, bọ ó rúbọ.

Translation:

a person had died

The settlers in heaven did not cry

A baby is born into the world

We are all the joy

The light of day is the night of the jinns

They were ones who launched Ifá for Alákòle

He who concealed the pain inside and pretended to be
happy while consulting Ifá

They asked him to offer sacrifice

he fulfilled

PROPHESY
Ifá says that there is a very influential man where this Odù

45

reveals himself, who is having a serious problem that he considers confidential and does not want anyone to know about him. Therefore, he is pretending to be happy, considering that he is far from being happy.

Ifá also says that there is a woman there, who can probably find the secret that the man had been jealously guarding from the beginning. Ifá warns that this woman should not try to reveal this secret, because if this secret is revealed, the shame will also affect the woman in question.

Ifá advised the man to offer sacrifice so he can solve his problem without exposing himself to public ridicule.

Ifá also says that the person who will help him solve his problem is a stranger whom he had not met. No one should lower their heads to any stranger, before whom you do not know. No one should lower their heads to any stranger where this Odù reveals himself.

Pataki

Alàkóle, the king of Ìkòlé-Èkìtì, had lost his sexual potency. He couldn't make love to his wives. Initially, the wives thought that they had offended their husband and he had decided to boycott them sexually. They pleaded with him to please the forgive. Taking a cue from the women's action, he refused to accept her plea. After several appeals, he informed them that he would think about it and communicate his decision after him to them.

Knowing that he could not continue to maintain this position, he went to the babalawo mentioned above for the ifa consultation. These babalawo tried to improve him but to no avail. This brought pain to Alakole but he continued to maintain a happy demeanor. He did not lose hope in ifa despite the failure of his babalawo. He kept his sadness inside and reported to no.

Ọpá ẹbí títè níí tẹ;

Kìí ṣé;

Díá fún Tẹẹtu;

Ọmọ wón ìnísà Òkè; níjọ́ tí wọ́n nlo rèé wẹẹ́ fun alákọlé;

Ọmọ alàgbá wòròwòrò ṣorò;

Wọn nó kó sákáalẹ, ẹbọ ni ṣíṣe;

Ó gbẹ́bọ, ó rúbọ

Translation:

The family unity rod can only be bent

must not break

he was the one who launched ifa for Tẹẹtu

The offspring of him to the Ìnísà-Òkè

When she would marry Alákòlé

He (alakole) who struck Agba furiously and repeatedly for the worship of Orò

They asked him to offer sacrifice

she fulfilled

As a result of Alakole's popularity and influence, the citizen of Inisa-Òkè reflected and decided to deal Tẹẹ́tu, a very pretty maiden, to him in marriage. Tẹẹ́tu then went to the babalawo mentioned above for the ifá consultation. They advised him to offer sacrifice of two guinea-fowl, two hens and money. She was also informed that she would be very happy in her matrimonial home. She was warned however that she should never expose her husband's secret to her. She complied. She then went to Alakole's house. She discovered her helplessness and fell silent.

Ìmọ-ìmọ sán kanlẹ, sán kàn'run

Awo igún ló díá fún igún

Igún Tóele ará ìlódò

Wọ́n ní kó sákáalẹ, ẹbọ ni ṣíṣe

Ó gbẹ́'bọ, ó rúbọ

Translation:

The lightening hit and touched the earth and sky

The awo of igún (vulture) was the one who launched Ifá for

Igún

Igún who prepared and prints ifá more than the settler of

the client's demand in the town of Ìlódò

They asked him to offer sacrifice

48

he fulfilled

Igún was a prominent Babaláwo in the town of Ìlódò. since the time he had decided to settle in this town things had not been moving well for him. Therefore, he approached the Awo mentioned above for Ifá consultation. They advised him to offer money sacrifice and perform Ifá ritual with two rats and two fish, palm oil, gin and money. He complied. He was sure that he would become a very successful man in that year, but he needed to leave Ìlódò to another community. It was during his stay that he would meet those who would invite him for lfa consultation and he would succeed where others had failed. The babalawo further informed him that the problem with the person who would make him a prosperous babalawo was that the person was having a secret illness that he did not wish others to know about. The client had been needing to offer sacrifice of two he-goats, two pants he had been wearing before, 20 kola nuts, 20 bitter kolas, palm oil, gin and money. He complied with the awo's advice and proceeded on the journey.

Meanwhile, Alákole had summoned his awo once more; they were the Òkú-ló-kú, ará-orun-ò sunkún; A bímo-láyé à nyo-seseese; Opá-ebí, Títe-níí-te, won-kìí-se. His main purpose was to find a solution to his impotence. Ogbè-gbàràdà was also revealed during the Ifá consultation.

Unfortunately, they couldn't identify Alakole's problem. Alakole then asked them to go far and wide in search of another babalawo who could identify his problem and offer a solution.

The awo scattered about in search of a babalawo who could solve the alakole problem. It was in this process that they met Igún. They were able to identify him as a babalawo because of the Idè that he put around his wrist and neck. He showed the Odù that they printed on the Ifá tray. Immediately Igún saw this Odù, he remembered his awo's instruction to them. He narrated to them exactly as he had been. They went to inform alakole. Alakole asked them on the other hand to go and bring Igun to his palace. They did. When Igun arrived at the Alakole Palace, he asked the Alakole to go and buy the prescribed sacrificial materials, he then entered the inner chambers of the Alakole Palace and all the necessary sacrifices were made. After this, the igun prepared all the medicines necessary to restore the potency of the alakoles beyond the alakole requirements. Briefly after, Alakole became sexually active again. Alakole was so happy that he made the main babalawo from him to igun.

We were all happy: Alákòlé, for recovering his power; The wives of Alákòlé, to be restored, with Alákòlé, babaláwo, to solve the problem of Alákòlé; Igún, to fit the babaláwo of the chief of Alákòlé, to be able to settle down and to become prosperous in life.

Òkú ló kú;

Ará ọrun ò sunkún;

A bímọ láyé;

À nyò sẹsẹẹsẹ;

Ọ́sán lòru ẹbọra eni;

Díá fún Alákọlé;

50

Ọmọ atìkùn sájà fara yíyña dífá;

Wón ni kó sákáalẹ, ẹbọ ní ṣíṣe;

Ó gbẹ́, bọ ó rúbọ;

Ọpá ẹbí títè níí tẹ;

Wọ́n Kìí ṣẹ́;

Díá fún Tẹẹ́tu;

Ọmọ wón ìnísà Òkè; níjọ́ tí wọ́n n lo rèé wẹẹ́ fun alákọlé;

Ọmọ alàgbá wòròwòrò ṣorò;

Wọn ní kó sákáalẹ, ẹbọ ni ṣíṣe;

Ó gbẹ́bọ, ó rúbọ;

Ìmọ-ìmọ sán kanlẹ, sán kàn'run;

Awo igún ló díá fún igún;

Igún Òtèlè ará ìlódò;

Wọ́n ṣẹṣẹ kó òhun Orò sílẹ;

Ni Igún wọlé dé;

Igún mà mà dé o

Translation:

a person had died

The settlers in heaven did not cry

51

A baby is born into the world

We are all the joy

Daylight is jinns night

They were ones who launched Ifá for Alákòle

He who concealed pain within and pretended to be happy

while Ifá called for consultation

They asked him to offer sacrifice

he fulfilled

The family unit rod can only bend

must not break

he was the one who launched ifa for T?? ?you

The offspring of him to the Ìnísà-Òkè

When she would marry Alákòlé

He (alakole) who struck Agba furiously and repeatedly for

the worship of Orò

They asked him to offer sacrifice

she fulfilled

The lightening hit and touched the earth and sky

must not break

¿He was the one who launched Ifá for you? you

The offspring of him to the oke of the inisa

When she would marry at alakole

He who struck the agba drum furiously and repeatedly for the cult of Orò

They asked him to offer sacrifice

she fulfilled

The lightening hit and touched the earth and sky

The awo De igún, was the one who launched Ifá for the igún

The igún awo (vulture) was the one whoe launched Ifá for Igún

Igún who prepared and prints ifá more than the settler of the client's demand in the town of Ìlódò

They asked him to offer sacrifice

he fulfilled

Igún, a settler in the town of ìlódò,

All the sacrificial materials had simply been procured

And Igun entered

Here comes Igun

He who prepares and prints ifá more than the client's demand, settler in the town of ìlódò.

Ifá says that all the people involved with you will be able to understand the desires of his heart. Ifá commands the babalawo, however, to always put the IDÈ on his wrist and the necklace on his neck.

ÒGBÈ ÒBÀRÀ VERSE 12

A kúnlẹ a yan Ẹ̀dá;

A dáyé tán, ojú n kán ni;

Enìkan kìí tún Ẹ̀dá yàn;

Àfi bí a tún Ayé wá;

Díá fún Ẹ̀dò;

Tíí se Òtukọ lát'Ọ̀run;

Wọn ní kó sákáalẹ ebo ní ṣíṣe;

Ò gbẹbọ, ó rúbọ

Translation:

(In the sky), we kneel and choose our fates

While, on earth, we are in a hurry

We can't change our destiny

Unless we reincarnate

These were the declarations of Ifá to Ẹ̀dọ

Who would pilot humanity from the sky

He was asked to offer sacrifice

he he fulfilled

PROPHESY
Ifá says that the person for whom this Odù is revealed must always remember his destiny. You should never be in too much of a hurry to succeed in life. Ifá also says that your client should look for a partner with whom to discuss everything you are starting in life, so the quality of your life will improve. Two good heads, people say, are better than one.

Pataki

Èdọ was in heaven. She wanted to participate in the business of piloting human beings from heaven to earth. Therefore, he went to the Awo mentioned above to determine how successful he would be if he participated in these businesses. He was asked to offer sacrifice of four white doves, four guineafowl, palm oil, gin and money. He complied. He was also advised to perform a ritual to his Orí with a guinea fowl, four kola nuts, four bitter kola and gin. He also complied. Since then, anyone he has piloted in the world would be very successful and prosperous, content and happy in life. On the other hand, those he did not pilot, no matter how hard they tried, would fail in life.

A kúnlẹ a yan Èdá;

A dáyé tán, ojú n kán ni;

Enìkan kìí tún Èdá yàn;

Àfi bí a tún Ayé wá;

Díá fún Ẹ̀dò;

Tíí se Òtukọ lát'Ọ̀run;

Wọn ní kó sákáalẹ ebo ní ṣíṣe;

Ò gbẹbọ, ó rúbọ; Kò pẹ, kò jìnnà;

Ẹ wá bá ni ní wọwọ Ire

Translation:

We kneel and choose our fates

While, on earth, we are in a hurry

We can't change our destiny

Unless we reincarnate

These were the declarations of Ifá to Ẹ̀dọ

Who would pilot humanity from the sky

He was asked to offer sacrifice

he he fulfilled

In a short time, not too long

We contemplate each other in the middle of everything Ire Ifá says that this person is good in the area of public relations, publicist, driving pilot, aviator pilot, merchant or other related areas. You can also dedicate yourself to writing the biographies of other people. You will be very successful in these fields. You will also be good as a musician or singer of praises, image washing and the like.

ÒGBÈ ÒBÀRÀ VERSE 13

Ogbè-Gbàràdá tán;

T'elégàn ló kù;

Ifá ṣe ohun gbogbo tán;

Ò ku ti ẹlẹun;

Díá fún Oníwọrọ-Òjé;

Ti yóó fọmọ lọkọ;

Ti iyá ò nìí gbọ;

Ti yóó fọmọ lọkọ;

Ti bàbá ò nìí gbọ;

Wọn ní kó sákáalẹ ẹbọ ní ṣíṣe;

Ò gbẹbọ, ó rúbọ

Translation:

Ogbè had performed wonders

Only the critics were not satisfied

Ifá had done everything to succeed, only the slander remained

These were the declarations of Ifá for Oníwòrò-Òjé

(the owner of the strings address)

Who will give a girl's hand in marriage

Without the knowledge of the girl's mother

Who will give a girl's hand in marriage

Without the knowledge of the girl's father

He was asked to offer sacrifice

she fulfilled

PROPHESY

Ifá says that there is a damsel where this Odù is revealed. Ifá says that if Ogbè-Gbàràdá is revealed for the selection of spouse or marriage purposes, the relationship between both parties will triumph. The condition under which it will happen is that the natural (blood) relatives of this lady must never be the ones to bestow the hand of her daughter. On the day that she will enter the house of her husband, her relatives should not pray for her. If possible, they should not take part in the marriage ceremony. They should leave all these activities to a family friend or neighbor who is not related by blood to the relatives of the lady in question. That is the only way that the relatives of this lady can realize the dreams of her daughter. If this is not done, the lady may die shortly after her dream is realized, or she will be unable to procreate her own children as long as her family lives. As an important matter, this lady should not go to her family's house until her first baby is born. She will then be able to

58

visit her family with her already born baby. This is very important and should be taken seriously.

Pataki

The family of the lady in question approached Oníwọrọ-Òjé after consulting the Babaláwo mentioned above for their daughter's marriage prospects. They were informed that they should not be the ones to conduct her daughter's marriage ceremony for her daughter's sake. They had to ask other people to come on her behalf. They were also advised to offer sacrifice of four pigeons, four guineafowl and money. They also had to perform an Ifá ritual with eight rats, eight fish, a guinea fowl, palm oil, gin and money. They complied. Después, abordaron a Oníwọrọ-Òjé para que permaneciera con ellos. Ella estuvo de acuerdo. Oníwọrọ-Òjé planeó la ceremonia de compromiso y el matrimonio actual sin informar a la familia de la niña.

A month after the marriage, the girl became pregnant. She gave birth to a vigorous baby. Later, she went to her family's house with her baby. It was joy and happiness all the way.

Ogbè gbàràdá tán;

T'ẹlẹgàn ló kù;

Ifá se ohun gbogbo tán;

Ò ku tẹlẹun;

Díá fún Oníwọrọ-Òjé;

Ti yóó fọmọ lọkọ;

Ti iyá ò nìí gbọ;

59

Ti yóó fọmọ lọkọ;

Ti bàbá ò nìí gbọ;

Wọn ní kó sákáalẹ ẹbọ ní ṣíṣe;

Ò gbẹbọ, ó rúbọ;

Njé Oníwọrọ-Òjé fọmọ lọkọ;

Iyà ò gbọ o;

Oníwọrọ-Òjé fọmọ lọkọ;

Bàbá ò gbọ; Oníwọrọ-Òjé ò, ire dé!

Translation:

Ogbè had performed wonders

Only the critics are not satisfied

Ifá had done everything to succeed

Only the calumnies remained

These were the declarations of Ifá for Oníwòrò-Òjé

(the owner of the strings address)

Who will give a girl's hand in marriage

Without the knowledge of the girl's mother

Who will give a girl's hand in marriage

Without the knowledge of the girl's father

He was asked to offer sacrifice

she fulfilled

Oníwọrọ-Òjé had given a girl's hand in marriage

The mother is not aware

Oníwọrọ-Òjé had given a girl's hand in marriage

The father is not aware

Oníwọrọ-Òjé, here deliver triumph and happiness!

Ifá says that the sequel to this action will be successful. Everyone involved will be happy if they can obey this important Ifa direction. The woman in question should not visit her family's home until after the birth of her first baby.

ÒGBÈ ÒBÀRÀ VERSE 14

Ogbè gbàràdá tán;

T'ẹlẹgàn ló kù;

Ifá se ohun gbogbo tán;

Ò ku tẹlẹun;

Díá fún Ọrúnmìlà;

Baba n lọ rèé fẹ Kúlúnbú;

Tíí S'omo Oba lóde Ìdó;

Wọn ní kó sákáalẹ ẹbọ ní şíşe;

Ọ gbẹbọ, ó rúbọ

Translation:

Ogbè had performed wonders

Only the critics are not satisfied

Ifá had done everything to succeed

Only the calumnies remained

They were the ones who launched Ifá for Òrúnmìlà

When she was planning to marry Kúlùnbú (A beautiful but young lady)

A princess in the Ìdó village

She was advised to offer a sacrifice

he he fulfilled

PROPHESY

Ifá says that there is a woman, where this Odù is revealed, who had a terrible attitude towards people, especially her husband. This woman is uneducated and she is unseemly. However, she destined to sire well-behaved children. If anyone plans to marry her, the person will know that the only thing he can gain from this woman is the kind of children he will give her. Other than this, she doesn't have anything that she is proud of. However, she has an influence from her house where her family are well behaved and very important in society. The woman in question is beautiful and short in stature.

Pataki

Òrúnmìlà asked the students mentioned above for an Ifá consultation when he was planning to marry Kúlúnbú, the princess of the Ìdó People. She was advised to offer a sacrifice with two pigeons, two guinea fowl, eight rats, eight fish and money. He was also advised to perform an Ifá ritual with a guinea fowl, palm oil and money. He complied. However, he was warned that Kúlúnbú was rude and short-tempered. She was also told that she would, however, give birth to humility, gentle leadership and the fear of God. The children that she will have will also be very successful in her life.

Òrúnmìlà, being someone of limited patience, preferred to marry Kúlúnbú with all her inconveniences for the children she would engender. In those days, children deserved more consideration than anything else. The Babaláwo said that everything would happen and Òrúnmìlà was very happy about it. He was giving praises to his students while they also worshiped Olódúmarè.

Ogbè gbàràdá tán;

T'ẹlẹgàn ló kù;

Ifá sehun gbogbo tán;

Ò kú tẹlẹnu;

Díá fún Ọrúnmìlà;

Baba nlọ rèé fẹ kúlúnbú;

Tíí sọmọ Oba lóde Ìdó;

Wọn ní kó sákáalẹ ẹbọ ní ṣíṣe o;

Ọ̀ gbẹbọ, ó rúbọ;

E jẹ ká fîse fóníṣe;

Kúlúnbú;

Ká fìwà fóníwà;

Kúlúnbú;

Ìgbà yí ni mo rí onítèmi o

Translation:

Ogbè had performed wonders

Only the critics are not satisfied

Ifá had done everything to succeed

Only the calumnies remained

They were the ones who launched Ifá for Òrúnmìlà

When she was planning to marry Kúlùnbú

A princess in the Ìdó village

She was advised to offer a sacrifice

he he fulfilled

Now, let us leave you with your character

Kúlúnbú

Let us tolerate their attitude

Kúlúnbú

Now is when I have found my choice.

ÒGBÈ ÒBÀRÀ VERSE 15

Ogbè gbàràdá tán;

T'ẹlẹgàn ló kù;

Ifá se ohun gbogbo tán;

Ò kú ti ẹlẹnu;

Díá fún Gáà;

A bù fẸṣin;

Àwọn méjèèjì jo nṣe ọrẹ òṣeyèkàn solùkù;

Wọn ní kí Gáà má yàá ẹnikẹni ní irù ìdíí rẹ;

Kò gbọ

Translation:

Ogbè had performed wonders

Only the critics are not satisfied

Ifá had satisfactorily complied with all things

Only the calumnies remained

They launched Ifá for Gáà. They launched the same for Ẹṣin

(a Horse)

The two of them were friends, but their friendship was as if they were brothers.

Gáà was warned not to lend his tail to anyone

He refused to heed the warning

PROPHESY

Ifá says that the person for whom this Odù is revealed, should not borrow anything from anyone, whatever it is that you cannot conclude, at the moment in which the person from whom you borrowed anything, you failed or refused to return it. Anything that you know is very precious to you, you should not give it to others because there is a great possibility that such object or thing will not be returned to you.

Pataki

Gáà and ballo were very close friends. Many people mistook their relationship because of how close they were. Both had been warned never to lend their property to anyone. They both complied.

However, one day the Horse would attend a dance competition. He had no tail. Only Gáà had a tail. The Horse asked Gáà to lend it to him. Gáà remembered Babaláwo's warning but preferred to ignore it for that time, claiming that the Horse was like his own brother and he would never refuse to return its tail after using it.

On the day of the dance competition, the Horse was the winner. Everyone told him how nice, how good it suited him and how beautiful the colé looked on the Horse. So the Horse decided never to return the colé. Gáà went to the Horse's house in order to claim his tail. The Horse abruptly refused to return Gáà's tail. This is how the Horse inherited the tail that originally belonged to Gáà. Before that, the Horse had no tail. He simply refused to return what belonged to another person, to the true owner of him. Gáà was very sorry for having refused to pay attention to Ifá's warnings.

Ogbè Gbàràdá tán;

T'ẹlẹgàn ló kù;

Ifá ṣe'un gbogbo tán;

Ò kú tẹlẹnu;

Díá fún Ẹ̀ṣin;

A bù fún Gáà;

Àwọn méjèèjì jo nṣòré ò seyèkàn solùkù;

Wọn ní kí Gáà má yàá ẹnikẹn ní irù ìdíí rẹ;

Kò gbọ;

Kò pé, kò jìnnà;

Ifá wá nṣe bí àlá mọrẹ

Translation:

Ogbè had performed wonders

Only the critics were not satisfied

Ifá had satisfactorily fulfilled all the things

Only criticism remained.

They launched Ifá for Gáà

They threw the same for the Horse

They were both friends, but their friendship was as if they

were partners

They warned Gáà about lending his tail to anyone

He refused to heed the warning

In a short time, not much

Ifá's warning happened as in a dream.

Ifá says that it is for the good of the client to desist from lending his belongings to people. Instead, you must give up anything that you might risk.

ÒGBÈ ÒBÀRÀ VERSE 16

Tìmùtìmù ab'àyà pi;

Díá fún Olókundé;

To nfomi ojú sùngbérèe tọmọ;

Wọn ní bó rúbo;

Yóó bìímọ;

Bí kò rúbo;

Yóó bìímọ;

Sùgbọn kó rúbọ kó leè bímọ;

Kó sì rúbọ kí àwọn ọmọ náà má di ọtá ara wọn;

Ẹbo kó bí'mọ nìkan ló rú.

Translation:

A ""mata"" with a strong chest (bravo)

He was the one who launched Ifá for Olókundé

Who was crying and lamenting over his inability to give birth

to children

He was informed that if he offered sacrifice

She should father children

If she refused to offer the sacrifice

She would father children

She was advised to offer sacrifice so that she might beget

useful children

And offer sacrifice so that the children do not become their

enemies

She only offered sacrifice to beget children

PROPHESY

Ifá says that the person for whom Ogbè-bàràdá is revealed needs to offer sacrifice in order to have good children and so that the children, when you have them, do not become your enemies.

Pataki

Olókundé was crying because she couldn't get pregnant. Then he approached Tìmùtìmù abàyà-pi for an Ifá consultation. She was informed that she had been destined to father children. However, she had to offer in sacrifice a ram and her underwear and her money so that the children would be born good and useful to her. She was also advised to offer three roosters as a sacrifice so that the children would not become her enemies in the future. Olókundé was desperate to have children and not be included in the group of sterile women. However, she sacrificed the black ram, her underwear and money, ignoring the sacrifice of the three roosters.

Shortly after the sacrifice, she Olókundé became pregnant and gave birth to Esin (Horse). Three years later, she became pregnant again and gave birth to Àfòn (African Fleshy Fruit). both were women.

Tìmùtìmù ab'àyà pi;

Díá fún Esin;

A bù fún Àfon;

Àwọn méjèèjì fẹyìntì ẹkún sùnráhùn ọmọ;

Wọn ní kí wón sákáalẹ̀, ebọ ní ṣíṣe;

Wọn ní bí wọn rúbọ;

Wọn yóó bìímọ;

Bí wọn ò rúbo;

Wọn yóó bìímọ;

Sùgbọn kí wọn rúbọ;

Kí wọn lè baà bímo;

Kí àwọn Òmọ náà má lè di ọtá araa wọn;

Ẹbo ọmọ nìkan ni wọn rú.

Translation:

A "mata"" with a strong chest

He was the one who launched Ifá for Esin (Horse)

He released the same for Àfọn (African Fleshy Fruit)

When both of them were crying and lamenting their inability to give birth to children

Both were advised to offer sacrifice

They were also informed that if they offered the sacrifice would give birth to children

71

If they did not offer the sacrifice

would give birth to children

However, they were advised to offer sacrifice, so they would have useful children.

And offer sacrifice, so the children would not be her enemies.

Both offered the sacrifice to give birth to children. When both Ẹṣin and Àfọn grew up and got married, they both had trouble giving birth. However, they went to the same Babaláwo with whom their mother went before they were born. They revealed the same Odù to her mother during the Ifá consultation. They were given the same advice. They also behaved exactly like their mothers by offering the sacrifice to give birth to children, but ignoring the sacrifice to prevent their children from becoming their enemies.

Shortly after, both Ẹṣin and Àfọn became pregnant. Àfọn gave birth first. During the naming ceremony, a small misunderstanding arose between Ẹṣin and Àfòn. Ẹṣin unintentionally trampled Àfọn's baby to death. Ẹṣin she gave birth to her own child, Àfọn came and poisoned the baby and the baby died. This is how Ẹṣin and Àfọn became enemies to this day. This was forever her repentance for refusing to offer the prescribed sacrifice.

Tìmùtìmù ab'àyà pi;

Díá fún Olókundé;

To fèyìntì mójú ẹkún sùnráhùn ọmọ;

Wọn ní kó sákáalẹ ẹbọ ní ṣíṣe;

Wọn ní bó rúbo;

Yóó bìímọ;

Bí ò rúbo;

Yóó bìímọ;

Sùgbọn kó rúbọ tọmọ;

Kó sì rúbọ kí àwọn ọmọ náà má di ọtá araa wọn;

Ẹbo ọmọ nìkan ló nṣe;

Ìgbà ti yóó bìí;

Ò bí Ẹṣin;

Ìgbà ti yóó bìí;

Ó bí Àfọn;

Tìmùtìmù abàyà pi;

Díá fún Ẹṣin;

A bù fún Àfọn;

Àwọn méjèèjì fẹyìntì mójú ẹkún sùnrahùn tọmọ;

Wọn ní kí wọn sákáalẹ ẹbọ ní ṣíṣe;

Wọn ní bí rúbo;

Wọn yóó bìímọ;

Bí wọn ò rúbo;

Wọn yóó bìímọ;

Ṣùgbọn kí wọn rúbo;

Kí wọn baà lè bímọ;

Kí awọn ọmọ náà má sì lé di ọtá araa wọn,

Ẹbọ ọmọ nìkan ni wọn rú;

Èrò Ìpo, èrò Òfà;

Ẹnìí gbẹ'bọ níbẹ kó ṣẹbọ o

Translation:

A "mata"" with a strong chest

He was the one who launched Ifá for Olókundé

Who was crying and lamenting over his inability to give birth
to children

He was informed that if he offered sacrifice

He would give birth to children

If he refused to offer the sacrifice

He would give birth to children

He was advised to offer sacrifice, so they would have useful
children

And offer sacrifice, so the children would not become his enemies.

She only offered sacrifice to beget children

She gave birth to Esin (Horse)

When she was to beget a child

She gave birth to Àfọn (African Fleshy Fruit)

A '''mata''' with a strong chest

He was the one who launched Ifá for Esin

She released the same for Àfọn

When both of them were crying and lamenting their inability to give birth to children

Both were advised to offer sacrifice

They were also informed that if they offered the sacrifice would give birth to children

If they did not offer the sacrifice would give birth to children

They were advised to offer sacrifice, so she could

Spawn useful children

And offer sacrifice, so the children would not be her enemies.

They only offered sacrifice to beget children

Travelers to Ìpo and Òfá

Leave those who were warned to fulfill the sacrifice.

3- OGBÈ ÒKÀNRÀN; OGBÈ KORAN; OGBÈ KÀNRÀN MÓLÈ

+

O	I
O	I
O	I
I	I

I PRAY:

Ògbè Òkànràn loda fún Ọbàtàlá loda fún Şàngó ni mi ti ala moni ala kosi moni yeun. Ògún bàbáré. Òrúnmìlà lorubo.

IFA OF:
• Disparagement

77

PROVERBS:
- Touch the Body
- The current is in the body
- Man disapproves of what he cannot do
- Death cannot, after eating a person's food, kill him.

BORN:
- The Board (Atepón of Ifá) and its secrets and the Irofá
- Where they took power away from Yèmoja
- Where they sacrificed Odùdúwà

- The Board with Irofá and brush

BRAND:
- Envelope of Spirits who want to take it before its time and against its will.
- That is why Ebo is made with: Corn, gbogbo Eré, 1 Adié, àṣo ará, o pò lo pò owó, it is sent to the cemetery and with the adié Paraldo (Body cleansing ritual) is made.

SIGNALIZE
- Ungrateful person.
- Big war that to win you need to ally with others.

IFÁ SAYS:
Say: Obàtàlá, Odùdúwà and Ṣàngó
- Odùdúwà who for being dominated by Éjìogbè, was crucified.
- Pulmonary congestion that ends with the person.
- A great war that to end it, you have to take Ṣàngó to the

78

patio for six days, put a red flag on him, blow otí on him and sound the Àṣeré
• The sensation of current flowing through of the person's body.
• That the mountain was believed to be very strong, but the sea was eating him for underneath until it collapsed.
• Of hidden diseases that come out at the moment.
• From hidden enemies working under
• That the person likes to masturbate.
• Ògbè Kana is born Bàbálawo, he works only Ifá.
• This Odù is to solve labor problems.
• From kneeling and Tetanus

PROHIBITIONS
• Do not be dominated by anyone, so that they do not discredit you
• Sick animals are not picked up on the street
• No one is picked up from your home, so that you don't hurt yourself.
• Do not go on walks or Masquerade balls
• Do not argue or dispute with anyone

RECOMMENDATIONS
• Dress in white, because your happiness is white clothes
• Beware of drafts and lung congestion.
• Bathe with: Sassafras, Almácigo, Ceiba, and Rompe Saragüey and then oborí with eight different fruits.
• Give eja tútù to Ṣàngó to solve at the foot of the Aragba tree
• Put a piece of Reef in the Ẹbọ
• For the woman, she has to Orugbo so that the damage does

not reach her and damages her womb and can have children.
- For the man: if the woman leaves, do not go looking for her.
- Receive ifá, because here the secrets of the Atepón de Ifá are born
- Give food to a deceased
- Give food to your head
- Serve your home and the saints (òrìşà)
- Put a Tuna behind the door
- Put a toy horse on your guardian angel.
- Tuna leaf

EWÉ ODÙ OGBÈ ÒKÀNRÀN

Tuna Espinosa	Cardón	Añil

For more information see: Encyclopedia of Ifá herbs by Marcelo Madan

PATAKI LISTING

1. The grateful evil. Thorns came out of the Tuna
2. The empowerment of Eegún when the children are born
3. The Heritage
4. The Elephant's Woman
5. Awó Moni Boşe was unhappy, because he did not listen to Şàngó's advice
6. The birth of the Irofá and the Board
7. The Òrìşàs tried to anger Obàtàlá
8. The path of the mountain and the Sea

WORKS WITH OGBÈ ÒKÀNRÀN

Work at the foot of Elégbà to ward off bad looks on me and

bad languages
You try to insert a prickly pear leaf on a piece of paper with the generals of the aráyé and it is lined in Aṣó funfun and pupa, but first a gio-gio (small chicken) is sacrificed to Elégbà and the prickly pear. Then the elenu (tongue) and oju (eye) of the gio-gio are pinned to the tuna. It is left at the foot of Elégbà until the situation is resolved.
Awo Ògbè Kana must plant a prickly pear around the house. A sea urchin is also put inside an igba and he stands in front of Elégbà and he is asked that the aráyé cannot reach.

Work to defeat the aráyé
For this Ifá according said Tata Gaitán (First head of Bàbálawos in Cuba), the work must be done at the foot of Ògún, because here, Ògún is stronger than all the others Òṣà.

Iṣé Òsányin for Àṣelú
A living Adam (bat), a dead one, Aṣó funfun and Dúdú, seven fox tail hairs. All done powder in two bags, one white and one black. Eat Aparó (quail). The white bag is used during the day and the black one at night.

Paraldo with a Goat
Element: A goat, a Rooster, a chicken for Paraldo, six candles, two coconuts, bouquet, Ìtanná, ekú, eja, Àgbado, efún, oyin, a bottle of otí, omiero casserole, two pound of Castile flour, food cooked, coffee, tobacco, etc.

For Eegún: Rice, sweet beans, soda, sweets, toys for the boys, a large gourd.

EWÉ (herbs): Añil, Albahaca Morada, Espanta Muerto, Sargazo, Algarrobo, Almácigo, Mar Pacífico, Escoba Amarga, Canutillo Morado.
(For more information around the herbs see: Encyclopedia of Ifá herbs by Marcelo Madan)

Iṣé Òsányin for Aṣelú
One Adam(bat) alive, one dead, aṣọ funfun and dundun, 7 hairs of Foxtail. All done I went in two bags, one white and one black. Come Apara. The white bag is used during the day and the black bag at night.

Paraldo with a goat
Element: A goat, a Pollón, a chicken for Paraldo, six candles, two coconuts, a bouquet, ìtanná, ekú, eja, Àgbado, efún, oyin, a bottle of otín, omiero casserole, two pounds of flour from Castilla, food cooked, coffee tobacco etc.
For Eegún: Rice, sweet beans, soda, candies, toys for the boys, a large gourd.

EWÉ: Indigo, Purple Basil, Espanta Muerto, Zargazo, Algarrobo, Almácigo, Pacific Sea, Bitter Escọba, Purple Canutillo.

Procedure:
1. An omiero is made
2. Obí omí tútù to Eegún
3. Place Elégbà in a position to put 60 mounds of flour from Castilla on each side in a straight line
4. Elégbà is given obí omí tútù and the goat and the chicken are slaughtered, giving Elégbà blood and the 120 little piles

of flour from Castile

5. The goat prepares to eat

6. In a large jícara, congrí rice is poured, the raw goat's head is added, along with all the preserves and the chicken from Paraldo, plus 120 mounds of flour from Castilla.

This jícara is taken to the bushy mountain, and a deity called Oloşe is called, giving an account of what has been done and that every year her food is going to be brought to her. After this a plate of everything that has been eaten and of all the sweets is taken out and all the boys are taken to the back of the house and the plate is given to the sick child in his hand and a procession is made with the children, from the back to the front with the sick child in front. The children exhorting and praising the boy to be called Apati, so that he eats.

Then everything is distributed to the children and the elderly, when the party is over the house is washed down with omiero.

To solve problems

A yucay bush is taken from the main root, threads of 7 colors are chalked inward and Yémọjá is placed asking it to resolve what one wishes, it is sung: Eyé petevi aro ifá petevi Olókun efe petevi Olókun ede me umpon ewa wo he. This is to call EFE, which is the spirit that protects Yémọjá and is the soul of the Manatee. In addition, Yémọjá is given 4 Eja tútù Bulls of the sea.

In this ifá, the face is washed with sugar water so that well-being and prosperity enters.

In this ifá, Yémọjá was stripped of the power to rule the

earth and she had to return to the sea where she became powerful again because the reefs where Saelo lived protected her from the araye of the earth. The Awó of this ifá always has to put a little piece of reef in the ẹbọ and in order to give power to the Yémọjá and her Olókun, he cannot lack a piece of reef inside her.

Jobs to attract:
If it is to attract a man: The name, soil from the shoe of the left foot, black and red thread, the name, 1gio-gio, epó, oyin, and a needle, 1ìtanná, 1 obí, at the foot of an Elégbà. If it is to attract a woman: Land of the right shoe, black and red thread, the name, 1 gio-gio, epó, oyin, 1 needle, 1 ìtanná, 1 obí, at the foot of Elégbà.

Lámpara para atraer al pie de Òṣùn

The complete general information of those interested is written on a piece of paper, it is put inso of Ologbo (Gata) ruin, igi, Yamao, Alamo, Amansa Guapo, it is well wrapped and chalked in yellow Oú (thread) and pupa. He is placed inside an igba and quicksilver, sweet wine, oyin, yellow precipitate, valerian powder, cooking oil is added to it and it is lit for 5 days at the foot of Òṣùn, it is taken to the river and there it is said:
Òṣùn Ìyá Me that, just as your waters run, that so-and-so himself runs after me. After Òṣùn grants it to him he is given two adié Aperí.

Work to defeat the Araye
For this Ifá, according to Tata Gaitan, the work must be

84

done at the foot of Ògún, because here Ògún is stronger than all the other Òṣàs.

Work at the foot of Elégbà to ward off bad views and tongues

A prickly pear leaf is placed on a piece of paper with the generals of the araye and is covered in aṣọ funfun and pupa, but before that a gio-gio is sacrificed to Elégbà and the prickly pear. Then the elenu and the oju of the gio-gio are pinned to the prickly pear. It is left at the foot of Elégbà until he resolves the situation.

Awo Ogbè Òkànràn must plant a prickly pear around the house. He also puts a sea urchin inside an igba and stands in front of Elégbà and asks that the araye not be able to reach the house.

Iṣé of Òsányin of Ogbè Òkànràn

Two iron screws, between one and the other, the names of the two people are put in ink on a Peregun sheet, the two screws are jammed with the Peregun sheet, with a string or hemp it is chalked and he gives ẹiyelé to him about Ògún, he wonders how many days he has to be there, then he gives it to the person, so that he can bury it in a flower pot.

Work for the Lungs

Take liver and heart, take a glass of this and another of cod liver oil and mix everything together, add a yolk of ẹyin adié, shake and drink once a day.

OGBÈ ÒKÀNRÀN PÀTAKI 1: THE GRATEFUL EVIL. THORNS CAME OUT OF THE PRICKLY PEAR.

Pàtaki

There was a time when the Prickly Pear had no thorns and lived between large and small trees and did not progress, because the animals when passing by it lay down to scratch and knocked it down, and also the children, in this situation it went to Òrúnmìlà's house lamenting what was happening to him. Òrúnmìlà made Osode for him and saw this ifá for him, and he immediately made a prayer for him. He began to make a series of incisions in which he later gave her eyebale, and with a preparation that he had, he began to put spikes in those incisions, as time passed when his children were born, they already had those thorns, so the enemies no longer approached them, and the family was able to prosper. But they were abandoned by their own families and went to live in the desert where no one bothered them. Once Òrúnmìlà was involved in a great war in which he was outmatched by the adversary, and in such circumstances, he remembered the favor he had done years before to the Tuna Brava and he went to her, since the survival depended on his help. victory. The Tuna, on the other hand, was indifferent to Òrúnmìlà's pleas and replied: It is not possible for me to help you, Òrúnmìlà, faced with such ingratitude, said: Truly, you are ungrateful, he reminded you of the favor that he had done you times ago, the Tuna upon hearing the recrimination that Òrúnmìlà rightly expressed, agreed to go with him to support him in his problem.

Note: The person you look at is bad, and he doesn't appreciate anything, and when he gets out of trouble, he forgets the favor they did him.

OGBÈ ÒKÀNRÀN PÀTAKI 2: THE EMPOWERMENT OF EEGÚN WHEN CHILDREN ARE BORN.

Pàtaki

There was a emaciated child because of his little food, and one day they gave him a party, the child was in his room lying down. A group of little friends gathered in the room, to whom a meal was offered, before eating they began to clap their hands singing: We want our little friend to eat. After they finished eating, they went to where their little friend was in the room and clapping their hands they sang: So-and-so, we want you to eat, let our little friend eat.
Earlier an Àkúko had been given to Elégbà.

EBQ:
Àkúko a Elégbà, gbogbo Tenuyen, give the children a meal and before and after eating they clap their hands and sing.

OGBÈ ÒKÀNRÀN PÀTAKI 3: THE HERITAGE.

EBQ:
Àkúko okàn, eiyelé méjì, igbin meyo, a jar, a piece of ivory, a bit of carob, cloth of different colors, orí, efún, ekú, eja, Àgbado, opolopo owó.

Pàtaki

A father lived in a town with his son who was single, and it happened that the father, seeing that he was going to die, called his son and said: I am poor and I can leave you nothing, but I would like you to get married as soon as possible, that I I assure you that you will be happy, if you do what I am going to tell you: When seven days have passed since my death, you will see that a worm comes out of my grave, catch it, that worm will transform into an Elephant, whom you will feed until it can fend for itself, then let it escape to the bush. With this buffalo horn that I give you, and these herbs, after the first seven months of each year, you will call the Elephant by blowing its horn, it will respond to your call and you will see how it grows, after five years, with the herbs that I give you they call the Elephant again, which you will tell him to go look for other Elephants and bring them to me, when you have gathered a large number of Elephants in the place that I tell you, you will make a large fence so that they cannot escape from there , then you bury the horn in a deep hole that you will later cover with earth, you will hunt one by one of these Elephants, and from their meat and tusks you will have riches, and the last one that remains is my meat, you can kill it but its remains will be distributed among your friends, you will not eat from it because it would be like eating yourself.

This is the inheritance that I can leave you, and saying this, he died. The son followed his advice and had riches in abundance.

OGBÈ ÒKÀNRÀN PÀTAKI 4 THE ELEPHANT WOMAN.

Pàtaki

Ate was the wife of the Elephant and one day Òrúnmìlà stole her, when he found out the Elephant was so outraged that he became furious and went out with the intention of killing Òrúnmìlà, this one who found out made ẹbọ with Tuna and loaded all his house with enough Tuna, when the Elephant came knocking down trees and when he arrived at Òrúnmìlà's house he attacked it so hard that the thorns were buried in his body, beginning to slap them to remove them from his body and the more effort he made the more he found out about them until fell dead. Òrúnmìlà came out and realized that he was dead, cut off his tail and fangs to make Irofá and began to sing.

OGBÈ ÒKÀNRÀN PÀTAKI 5 AWO MONI BOṢE WAS UNHAPPY BECAUSE HE DIDN'T LISTEN TO ṢANGO'S ADVICE.

I Pray:
Ogbè Òkànràn Awó ni bebe ni lórun Awó Boni Boṣe abelekun lórun Inlé ganga ni lo e bani láye Inlé borele Oní ofoto mi yo ni Ṣàngó ọmọ Awó Moni Boṣe Olórun Ṣàngó Ogbè Òkànràn Ṣàngó odara.

ẸBỌ:
Eja tútù, Akuaró, gbogbo Eré, igi Araba, an òtá, otín, ataré méta, oyin, opolopo orí, Àgbado, owó.

Note: The owner of this sign can never be separated from Ṣàngó, to overcome difficulties, for this ifá you always have to give Eja tútù to Ṣàngó.

Pàtaki:

On this road in the Ganga ni Lode land, lived an Awó son of Ṣàngó called Moni Boṣe, said Awó had a lot of work to direct the land, because good results were not seen from everything he ordered and spoke. His people began to get sick and the problems among the inhabitants were increasing, all this happened to Awó Moni Boṣe because his father was always advising him to stick to him and not listen to his mother's advice that in this sign was called Eni Ofo Temo llo, which had taught her son Moni Boṣe nothing but everything bad, she had him as if he were a slave, because of the selfishness that no one else was by his side, he could not have happiness with no woman and every time he had one, his mother Eni ọfò Tem illo, went to the secret that she had, which consisted of an òtá and called it in this way: Totori lala Eni ọfò Tomi llo Ìyá Awó Boni Boṣe Obìrin ọfò, oreran lerí Awó Moni Boṣe.
She smeared Epó on the òtá and covered it with a black cloth and the Obìrin that Awó Moni Boṣe had began to dodge and abandoned him.

All this problem had Ṣàngó very worried to see that his son did not listen to his advice and was followed by his mother. One day Ṣàngó caught a Paṣan, Ero and with a white hen called the secret of Eni ọfò Tomillo in this way: Oní Lele mafun Oporogun Awó Moni Boşe Maliye Ibare Lekun Láye Ìyá Awó Moni Boşe. And he gave the òtá eyebale of the Adié funfun, the Ìyá of Mono Boşe began to feel stunned when he took advantage of Şàngó and took him to the land of Ganga ni Lode, to govern that town and forget about his mother to be someone in life, you have to learn even if it costs you a lot of work you will lead this land, and your mother's influence will always come to you, that's why you have to stick to me that I am the only one who can save you. Awó Moni Boşe did not hear Şàngó and continued with her thoughts fixed on her mother, that is why in the Ganga ni Lode land everything was backwardness and illness, once the entire population gathered in front of Awó Moni Boşe's house, to ask her to saved him from so much epidemic and delay, he said he would call Şàngó his father, so he did and Şàngó immediately responded to his call and went with his son to earth, when they saw them arrive the population was very happy, thinking that Şàngó could help, Awó Moni Boşe sent him messages of works and jobs for his people, but his people got worse, the sick began to die and vice versa, all this was due to the action of Şàngó who was creating problems for His son, for he did not want to hear it, seeing this misfortune Awó Moni Boşe threw himself to cry at the feet of Şàngó he asked for forgiveness and told him: That he would obey him in everything, that he forgive his mother so that she can perform a ceremony for me, when the Ìyá and seeing his son so destroyed he asked for forgiveness and told him, that m ás would never touch the secret of the òtá and to forgive her for being so selfish and harsh with him, Awó Moni Boşe forgave her and said to Şàngó: What is the ceremony I have to do to return to the land Ganga ni Lode

91

and save her , Şàngó told him: Look for an Eja tútù and next to a Ceiba call me well and give it to me together with your lerí.

Prayer: To give Eja tútù to Şàngó with the lerí.
Salara ordo ni ifá Awó Moni Boşe abeyemi ifá kori bo wo ayé oni lórun Odduwa Òrúnmìlà awa Ifá´moyare odara ifá Şàngó aguani lórun.

Iyere: Eja to lerí

Eyé Eyeni Lerí Aragba Feleguegue Awa Boreo.

When Awó Moni Boşe finished the ceremony, Şàngó put his hands on his head and told him: Now go to the land that little by little you will save, although there will always be problems and illnesses To Iban Èşù.

OGBÈ ÒKÀNRÀN PÀTAKI 6: THE BIRTH OF THE IROFA AND THE BOARD.

Pàtaki

At the beginning of the creation, Òrúnmìlà was a close friend of the Elephant and he entered the mountain with him and together they did all kinds of tasks to look for some money and thus earn their daily livelihood, but Òrúnmìlà did not have the same strength as the Elephant, he could not work like him. They worked together in the bush for three months and three consecutive years, but when they finished, Òrúnmìlà had little money and only his money was enough

92

to buy a white suit, however, Ayanaku (Elephant) had earned a lot of money.

On the way to the city, Òrúnmìlà told Ayanaku: We are going back to work in the mountains to earn more money, the Ayanaku replied: You can come back if you wish, because I earned enough money. As Òrúnmìlà had little money that he had spent on his white suit, he returned to the mountain, but first he gave his white suit to Ayanaku so that he could take it to his house and keep it until his return. When Òrúnmìlà returned from the mountain with a little more money, he met the Elephant who was wearing his white suit and when asked about it, he replied: You have never given me anything to keep, both fought, but Òrúnmìlà did not he was able to defeat the Elephant because he was much stronger than Òrúnmìlà, and because of that they separated. Òrúnmìlà took Ado's path without his white suit and the Elephant took Alo's path with his white suit on, on Ado's path Òrúnmìlà met a head that told him that he was hunting an Elephant, Òrúnmìlà He replied: I just saw one dressed in white that took the path of Alo. The hunter went that way and when he saw the Elephant, he killed it with his arrows, opened it and found its white pouring inside, then cut off its leri, tail and tusks, and took it to Òrúnmìlà as a present. Then Òrúnmìlà with the tail made the Iruke, with the fang he made the Irofá and with the front he made the Board.

Note: The White dress is the wing, the intestinal mantle of animals.

GBE ÒKÀNRÀN PÀTAKI 7 EVERYTHING IS ASKED TO IFÁ.

Pàtaki

Òrúnmìlà went out for a walk and arrived at a farm where there were some bushes with very precious fruits, which were poisoned because the people of that town were at war with another town and were waiting for him to see if they would be poisoned with the fruits, because of that way it was easier to fight with opponents. Òrúnmìlà, ignoring this situation, jumped over the fence and reached the bottom of the bush, plucked fruits from it and began to eat. The people of that town, seeing him eating those fruits, yelled at him: Hey, don't eat that fruit, they are poisoned, but it was too late because Òrúnmìlà had eaten them and poisoned himself, for getting into other people's places without first asking.

4- TRADITIONAL IFA ÒGBÈ OKANRAN

ÒGBÈ OKANRAN VERSO 1

Koi san won

Koi ro won

Awo Ologonsese

Dia fun Ologonsese

Tii nsehun Gbogbo

Ti okan ko loju

Ebo ni won ni ko waa se

O gb'ebo, o rubo

Koi san won o

Awo Ologonsese

Nigba o ba ma san mi o

Ma mu iyun Sode

Translation

still not comfortable

And they are still not satisfied

The Awo of Ologonsese

They cast Ifa for Ologonsese

When I was doing all things without achieving any

She was advised to offer ebo   '

fulfilled

still not satisfied

The Awo of Ologonsese

As soon as I feel comfortable

I will use coral to make my own Ide

1.   Ifá says that the person for whom this sign was revealed has to adorn their wrist, waist and neck with Ifá beads, so that you have peace of mind and tranquility in your life. Ifá says that he is your protector and sanctuary. Ifa will make this person carry Ifa on their head and display it anywhere they go. Ifá advises this person to offer ebo with

two roosters, two hens, eight rats, eight fish and money. You also need to feed Ifá according to the case and make sure that you have the Ide of Ifá in his person at all times.

ÒGBÈ OKANRAN VERSO 2

Okanrán Sode lo galanja

Dia fun Orunmila

Para limpiar Apetebi aya oun o yun

Ebo ni fun ni ko waa se

O gb'ebo, o rubo

Oojo aya Awo ba Sode

Aya Awo un soyun

Translation

Okanrán Sode galanja it

Ifá's message for Orunmila

When he lamented that his Apetebi had not received the

blessing of the fruit of the womb

He was advised to offer ebo

fulfilled

The day the Awo's wife tied the Ide

The Awo's wife will be blessed with pregnancy

2. Ifá advises a sterile woman to tie the Ide cord of Ifá so that she receives the blessing of the fruit of the womb. Ifá says that this woman is an Apetebi. Ifá advises you to offer ebo with four chickens, eight rats, eight fish and money. After this, she has to feed Ifá with the rat and the fish.

ÒGBÈ OKANRAN VERSO 3

Afakara p'odi awo ile Elesire

Dia fun Elesire isaaju

Nijo tin sea laarin edidi

Ti nbe laarin ota

Ebo ni won ni ko waa se

O gb'ebo, o rubo

Mo gboku odi mo rin won o

Mo gboku odi mo rin won o

Afakara podi Lawo Elesire Isaaju

Mo gboku odi mo rin won

Translation

The one who uses akara to eliminate his enemy

The resident Awo of elesire

98

Launched Ifá for Elesire isaju

When he was in the middle of antagonist

And he was in the midst of enemies

He was advised to offer ebo

fulfilled

I had the death of the enemy

and i laughed

The one who uses akara to eliminate enemies

She is the Awo of Elesire Isaju

I had the death of enemies and I laughed

3   Ifá advises the person for whom this sign is revealed to offer the ebo of victory over the adversary. Ifá says that this enemy will die a shameful death, if he does not desist from attacking the person for whom this odu is manifested. Ifá advises that person to offer ebo with 200 Akara, 3 guinea fowl and money. For 16 days of this Ifá consultation, you need to feed Ifá with a mature goat.

ÒGBÈ OKANRAN VERSO 4

Orunmila lo di kutukutu nsode

Ifa mo lo di werewere ndade

Ifa ni Apetebi pale Edu tabi ko pale

Won ni Apetebi pale

Ifa ni to ba pale

Yoo nii gurukan inu

Orunmila lo di kutukutu nsode

Ifa mo lo di werewere ndade

Ifa ni Apetebi pale Edu tabi ko pale

Won ni Apetebi pale

Ifa ni to ba pale

Yoo nii gurukan eyin

Orunmila lo di kutukutu nsode

Ifa mo lo di werewere ndade

Ifa ni Apetebi pale Edu tabi ko pale

Won ni Apetebi pale

Ifa ni to ba pale

Yoo nii gberumi-somi

Oyun ni gurukan inu

Omo ni gurukan eyin

Eru ni gberumi-somi

Orunmila Ela-sode

Ifa je nni gberumi-somi ninu agbo

Translation

Orunmila declares that early in the morning we tie the Ifa cord

I declare that they also adorn our wrist with brass ornaments

Orunmila asks if Apetebi takes proper care of the Ifa room or not

They reply that Apetebi really does take proper care of the Ifa room

Orunmila says that if she takes care of the Ifa room

She will be blessed with the fruit of the womb

Orunmila declares that early in the morning we tie the Ifa cord

I declare that they also adorn our wrist with brass ornaments

Orunmila asks if Apetebi takes proper care of the Ifa room or not

They reply that Apetebi really does take proper care of the Ifa room

Orunmila says that if she takes care of the Ifa room

She will be blessed with the baby on her back

Orunmila declares that early in the morning we tie the Ifa cord

I declare that they also adorn our wrist with brass ornaments

Orunmila asks if Apetebi takes proper care of the Ifa room or not

They reply that Apetebi really does take proper care of the Ifa room

Orunmila says that if she takes care of the Ifa room

She will be blessed with the various maidens and servants

Orunmila ela Sode

Please let me be blessed with the three among Awo

4. Ifá asks a woman seeking the blessing of the fruit of the womb to offer ebo with a mature goat, eight rats, eight fish and money. Ifá assures this woman that all she has to do is take proper Ifá care that no medicine will ever work for her.

ÒGBÈ OKANRAN VERSO 5

Okeere fefe la Gboro egan

Dia fun Oja

Tii sí Iya Aro

Ebo ni won ni ko waa se

O gb'ebo, o rubo

Bi o ba si Oja

Eye niba yoju Aro loko

Translation

It's from the distance that we hear the desert rumble

Ifá's message for Oja

Who was Aro's mother

She was advised to offer ebo

she obeyed

If it wasn't for Oja

Birds would have removed Aro's eyes for consumption on
the farm

5. Ifá says that there is a person where this sign is revealed,
who has a very terrible character. You misbehave the way
you like. Fortunately for you, however, everyone who could
have treated you ruthlessly was considering the person's
mother's good character and that they were being lenient
with you. Ifá, however, warns that this person changes her
character forever, so that the world will not descend on you.
Ifá advises this person to offer ebo with a mature goat and
money. You also need to feed Ifá with a mature ram and
feed Shangó with another ram. Ifá says that the internal
organ of the three animals must be used to feed the elders
of the night. No matter what this person uses as ebo

material, however, you will have to change for the better.

ÒGBÈ OKANRAN VERSO 6

A Kii somo Babalawo ka binu

A Kii somo onisegun ka saigbodoran

A Kii somo Baale ka baluu je

Dia fun Adekannbi

Tii somo Okanrán-Sode

Ebo ni won ni ko waa se

O gb'ebo, o rubo

Adekannbi omo Okanrán-Sode

Mo gbo wipe Awo nsode

Mo ba won ase o

Translation

We cannot be a son of a babalawo and display anger

We can't be the son of a herbalist and show stubbornness

And we can't be the son of the community leader and mess up the community.

Ifá's message for Adekanbi

Okanran Sode's son

He was advised to offer ebo

fulfilled

now adekanbi

Okanran Sode's son

I found out that the Awo is tying the Ifa cord

And I join them in tying mine

6. Ifá says that the person for whom this sign was revealed must learn to exercise patience and self-limitation at all times. Ifá says that it is the excessive anger that this person was to be used to ruin his destiny. With patience, humility and meekness, heaven is the beginning of this person's success in life. Ifá advises that person to offer ebo with four guinea fowl, four hens, four pigeons, four roosters and money. There is also the need to feed Ifa with an adult pig.

ÒGBÈ OKANRAN VERSO 7

Wiriwiri-ki

Dia fun won Leku Otún

Won nsunkun awon o laje lowo

Won ni Eegun ilee Babayin ni kee bo

Wiriwiri-ki

Dia fun won Leku Osi

Won nsunkun awon o bimo

Won ni Eegun ile Baba yin ni kee bo o

won gb'ebo, won rubo

Wiriwiri-ki! Owo de

Wiriwiri ki! Aya de

Wiriwiri ki! Omo de

Translation

Wiriwiri-ki

The Ifá message for the inhabitant of the part of the stream on the right

When they were lamenting their inability to secure financial success

They were advised to go and propitiate Egungun in their father ancestral lineage

Wiriwiri-ki

The Ifá message for the inhabitant of the creek on the left

When they were lamenting their inability to secure the fruit of the womb

They were advised to go and propitiate Egungun in their father ancestral lineage

both meet

now wiriwiriki

the money has arrived

Wiriwiriki

husband had arrived

Wiriwiriki

the babies have arrived

7. Ifá advises the person for whom this sign is revealed, to feed the Egungun of his paternal lineage, with a mature ram. Ifá says that one person is in need of financial wealth, while another person is desperately praying for the fruit of the womb. Each of them has to offer ebo with a mature ram and feed Egungun with another mature ram.

ÒGBÈ OKANRAN VERSO 8

Ide ti mo pecado ni isin-nsin

Ide ti mo ra ni ira-nra

Ide ti mo lo niso-nsomowo

Omo eku wole eran

Omo eku Gbe o lo

Omo eja wole eran

Omo eja lo Gbe o

Omo Eran wole eran

Omo Eran Gbe o lo

Orunmila lo d'abo

Mo lo dade

Mo ni a ba dabo toa dede nko

Moni kini a ti o maa somo eku

Moni kini a ti o maa somo eja

Moni kini a ti o maa somo ojo

Moni kini a ti o maa somo Eran

Onikoo maa fomo eku boke Ipori oun ni

Onikoo maa fomo eja boke Ipori oun ni

Onikoo maa fomo ojo boke Ipori oun ni

Onikoo maa fomo Eran boke Ipori oun ni

Ifa sí tan, Ifa ndari omo eku je

Ifa sí tan, Ifa ndari omo eja je

Ifa sí tan, Ifa ndari omo eye je

Ifa sí tan, Ifa ndari omo Eran je

Ide ti mo pecado ni isin-nsin

Ide ti mo ra ni ira-nra

Omo eni wole eran

Omo eni eni lo gbede o

Orunmila lo dabo, mo lo dade

Mo ni Kinla o ti maa somo eni

Orunmila ni omo eni naa nii gbede eni lo

Omo ni yoo gbede wa o

Omo eni ni yoo gbede eni o

Baba a mi wi

Mo gbede e re

Omo eni ni yoo gbede eni o

Translation

The lace Ide you tie in the way you suppose it should be tied

And the Ide beads I bought in the form of an Ide lanyard

are supposed to be bought

The Ide cord that I tied around my wrist

A rat snuck in quietly and took him

Orunmila declare that everything is left until he returns

And in chorus that everything will happen when I return

The Orunmila requested

What do you think will happen when I return

Orunmila declare that she will use the rat as food material

for her Ifa

The lace Ide you tie in the way you suppose it should be tied

And the Ide beads I bought in the form of an Ide lanyard

are supposed to be bought

The Ide cord that I tied around my wrist

A fish sneaked up silently and took him away

Orunmila declare that everything is left until he returns

And in chorus that everything will happen when I return

The Orunmila requested

What do you think will happen when I return

Orunmila declare that he will use the fish as food material
for his Ifa

The lace Ide you tie in the way you suppose it should be tied

And the Ide beads I bought in the form of an Ide lanyard

are supposed to be bought

The Ide cord that I tied around my wrist

A bed sneaked quietly and took it away

Orunmila declare that everything is left until he returns

And in chorus that everything will happen when I return

The Orunmila requested

What do you think will happen when I return

Orunmila declare that he will use the bird as food material
for his Ifa

The lace Ide you tie in the way you suppose it should be tied

And the Ide beads I bought in the form of an Ide lanyard

are supposed to be bought

The Ide cord that I tied around my wrist

A silent beast sneaked up and took him away

Orunmila declare that everything is left until he returns

And in chorus that everything will happen when I return

The Orunmila requested

What do you think will happen when I return

Orunmila declare that he will use the beast as food material

for his Ifa

The lace Ide you tie in the way you suppose it should be tied

And the Ide beads I bought in the form of an Ide lanyard

are supposed to be bought

The Ide cord that I tied around my wrist

Some child entered the house and understands the languages

Our children will understand our language

when my father dies

I understood your language

That our children understand our language

8. Ifá advises the person for whom this sign was revealed to

tie the Idé beads on her children. You also have to show the children the path of Ifa at all times. You must also give these children the best training so that these children are going to listen to you all the time. Ifá advises this person to offer ebo with two rats, two fish, two birds, two beasts and money.

ÒGBÈ OKANRAN VERSO 9

Gbemi gedegede ki n ma tese bo'mi

Dia fun Orunmila

Ifa nlo re Gbe Ide niyawo

Ebo ni won ni ko waa se

O gb'ebo, o rubo

E wa ewa womo Ide Weere

Afedefeyo, Edu ti gbe'De niyawo

E wa, wa e womo Ide Weere

Translation

Take me for me not to touch the water with my legs

Ifá's message for Orunmila

When she is going to have Ide for woman

She was advised to offer ebo

fulfilled

Come and see the many sons of Ide

Afedefeyo Edu has married Ide by wife

Please come and see the many children of Ide

9. Ifá says that she foresees an iré from a compatible spouse for the person to whom this sign is revealed. The couple will produce many children of their own through this relationship. Ifá advises them to offer ebo with four rats, four fish, two chickens and money.

ÒGBÈ OKANRAN VERSO 10

Hunnuhunnu lota see ro

Hun nuhunnu nilo see kan

Ota Kii fibi riro pa Babalawo

Odu Kii ye ko p'awon agba isegun

Dia fun Olofin ti won nse-hun hun hun-le lori

Ebo ni won ni ko waa se

O gb'ebo, o rubo

Nje Esuo igbo o

Ekulu odan

Etu ni yoo ba mi tumo o rikisi

Orin nii tu'mo enu

Gbongbo ona nii tumo ese

Ataare nii tumo awon isegun

Bosan-un bautismo en o, imo eni ni a tu

Esuo igbo o, ekulu odan

Etu ni yoo ba mi tumo o rikisi

Translation

Hunnuhunnu burbot see ro

Hun nuhunnu nile see kan

The rock cannot collapse to kill a babalawo

An Odu cannot kill a great herbalist

Ifá's message for Olofin

Who people are conspiring against

He was advised to offer ebo

Now Esu of the desert

And ekuru from the savannah region

Etu the antelope will help disperse all your conspiracies

It is the chewing stick that disperses conspiracies in the mouth

Y is the root that crosses the root path

The scattered conspiracies of the feet

I will tie the guinea pepper that are scattered by the conspiracy of the herbalist

When it's evening time the dew conspiracy will scatter

Esu of the forest and ekuru of the savannah earth

Let etu help me disperse all your conspiracies

9.   Ifá says that the person for whom this sign was revealed has many people who conspire against him. Ifá, however, assures him a resounding victory over the entirety of this town. Ifá advises that person to offer ebo with three roosters and money. After this, this person goes to find Esu's skin, Antelope, Etu's skin, Antelope, Ekulu's skin, ram bush, a bunch of chewing stick, a bunch of crocodile pepper. The root of a tree crossing the road, a droplet of dew. The dew drop will be collected in a container. All remaining items are beaten together and mixed with soap and water. The dew drop can be used as water to mix the soap properly. The person to whom this sign is revealed uses the soap for bathing and an incision will also be made on his head with the soap.

ÒGBÈ OKANRAN VERSO 11

ÒGBÈri Itage fohun olola

Dia fun Orunmila

Tii yoo soko Eyele

Ti yoo soko Adie

Tii yoo soko Ewure

Ebo ni won ni ko waa se

O gb'ebo, o rubo

Obajio, bolso mo bi ser o nide ree

Kide o lo Lorun mi dogbodogbo

Amo bi o mo ba Gbe o nide ree

Kide o ma so Lorun mi dogbodogbo

Translation

The one who stayed on stage and act like an influencer

Ifá's message for Orunmila

Who will be Eyele's husband

The one who stayed on stage and act like an influencer

Ifá's message for Orunmila

Who will be Adie's husband

The one who stayed on stage and act like an influencer

Ifá's message for Orunmila

Who will be the husband of Ewure

The day they stole is Ide lanyard

She was advised to offer ebo

fulfilled

Obajio, if I was the one who stole his Ide lanyard

Let the Ide form a knot in the neck

But if I didn't steal your Ide lanyard

Let the Ide stop forming a knot in the neck

11. Ifá says that there are some women that this sign is revealed and one of them had stolen something that belongs to the head of the family. Ifá says that the person that everyone suspected of the theft is not the person who had stolen what they were looking for. Ifá says that the thief will soon be exposed and ashamed. However, it is in the best interest of the person who stole what they were looking for to confess and return the stolen item. Ifá advises this person to offer ebo with a mature goat and money.

ÒGBÈ OKANRAN VERSO 12

Sango n gb'ara Oyo

Yemoja n gb'ara ojo

Awon Onsoña n gb'Onibode Ife

Dia fun Orunmila

Ti nloo ra Arikusaba-Ogogo leru

Ebo ni won ni ko waa se

O gb'ebo, o rubo

Ito ti Onigboori que won o l'aare

Onigbigbo, Gbogbo yin le je Baba

Alaaja, baba ni

Ojamba baba ni

Pekepeke baba ni

Baba-Lagure baba ni

Awon Arikusaba-Ogogo ni ganó da un buen presagio sile

Won ni ki Gbogbo aye o ba maa won naa

Ito onigboori que won o l'Aare

Oribigbo, Gbogbo yin le je baba o

Translation

Sango is compatible with the inhabitants of the city of Oyo

Yemoja supports the inhabitants of the farm

The antisance support the sentinels on Ile Ife

Ifá's message for Orunmila

When will Arikusaba Ogogo buy as a slave

So big and his Onigbori his have no leader

Oribigbo all of you are leaders

Alaaaja is leader

Ojanba is a leader

pekepeke is leader

Babalagure is leader

118

It is arikusaba Ogogo people who started the work of border guards

They invited everyone to come and participate

As big as onigboyi is they have no leader

Oribigbo all of you are leaders

12. Ifá says that the first business that the person for whom this Odu is revealed will undertake will make you very sad and uncomfortable in the initial stage, in the end you will be supposed to smile and celebrate. This is why this person has to be patient, persistent, and consistent. You should not appear at any time anger or impatience. Ifá advises this person to offer ebo with four rats, four fish, two pigeons, two chickens, two guinea fowl, two roosters and money.

ÒGBÈ OKANRAN VERSO 13

Agbe nii tibi didii g'odan

Aluko nii tibi ReeRee g'osun

Eje omo titun ni o ro-gbaara gbooro ninu Awo tannganran

Dia fun Asode-ma-gbofa

Ti nsawo rele Olofin

Ebo ni won ni ko waa se

O gb'ebo, o rubo

Translation

Agbe the blue touracco is what perches on Odan trees from the thickest part of the tree

Aluko, the brown turacco is the one that falls on Osu tree

The blood of a newborn baby does not flow in a dish

The Ifá message for the one who ties the Ide cord without having a deep knowledge of Ifa

When they went on an Ifa mission to Olofin palace

He was advised to offer ebo

fulfilled

In a short time and not too far

Join us in the midst of all life Ire

13. Ifá says that there is a babalawo where this Odu is revealed, who is paying to put on the Idé and the necklace around his wrist and his neck. This babalawo is not well versed in Ifá. But Ifá warns the association or group of babalawo that they should never drive away this particular babalawo, as a result of their lack of deep knowledge of Ifá. If they do, everyone will meet with disgrace and humiliation. Ifá also advises this babalawo to behave like a true child of Ifá at all times. Ifa will always come to support him. Ifá advises that ebo can only be offered with two pigeons, two chickens, two guinea fowl, two roosters and money. You also need to feed Ifa accordingly.

ÒGBÈ OKANRAN VERSO 14

Ila sowo deere, ila sogun

Ikan sowo deere sogbon

Agbon Oyinbo nii soros yetuyetu bi ori omo titun

Dia fun Ata

Ti nloo ba won setutu n'Ife

Ebo ni won ni ko waa se

O gb'ebo, o rubo

Ada o gbofa o

Etutu l'Ada mo

Awo rere lo metutu

Translation

The okra tree extended its branch and 20 seeds germinated

The egg orchard tree spread its own branch and germinated 30

The pineapple has plumes on its head like that of a newborn baby

Ada's Ifa message

When will the ritual be performed in Ife

He was advised to offer ebo

fulfilled

Ada is not versed in Ifa

But Ada understands how to perform etutu rituals

A good and competent Awo knows how to perform Etutu

14. Ifá promises that the person for whom this sign is revealed will be given authority in life. Ifá says that everything you say was accepted and done like this is going to happen. Ifá says that this person became an influential and important personality in the community. Ifá advises this person to offer ebo with four rats, four fish, two chickens, two pigeons, two guinea fowl, two roosters and money. You also need to feed Ifá, either with a chicken or a guinea fowl or a goat.

ÒGBÈ OKANRAN VERSO 15

Yunyun nii nii Gboko dade Ori

Ookun gidigba nii rin taraare-taraare

Dia fun koiromi

Tii somo Ologunsese

Igbati a njaye inira kaka

Ebo ni won ko waa se

O gb'ebo, o ru'bo

Ko pe, ko jinna

E ba ni bayo

E waa wo're

Translation

Yunyun tree remains in the forest and wears a crown

The mature millipede is the one that works alone

Ifá's message for koiromi, I'm still not comfortable

The AWO by ologunsese

When I was in the midst of untold suffering

She was advised to offer ebo

fulfilled

Travelers to Ipo and the Land Ofa

Join us in the midst of joy

Come and feel all the wrath of life

15. Ifá says that the person for whom this sign was revealed is currently suffering and that he is finding everything difficult. Ifá assures this person that he will soon smile and all his sufferings will soon become a thing of the past. Ifá advises that person to offer ebo with two rats, two fish, two pigeons, two chickens, two guinea fowl, two roosters and money. You also need to feed Ifa with a guinea fowl.

ÒGBÈ OKANRAN VERSO 16

Okanrán Sode lo galanga

Dia fun Orunmila

Baba nlo ajo a jin gbooro bi ojo

Ebo ni won ni ko waa se

O gb'ebo, o ru'bo

Ko pe, ko jinna

E ba ni latule ire Gbogbo

Translation

Okanrán Sode galanga him

Ifá's message for Orunmila

When going on an Ifa mission to a long distance land

He was advised to offer ebo

fulfilled

In a short time, not far

Join us in the midst of success

16. Ifá assures the person for whom this sign was revealed, that he will travel to another field in business and that you will succeed beyond his greatest dream. Ifá advises this person to offer ebo with four pigeons, four chickens and money. You also need to feed Ifá, either with a goat or a pig.

124

5- VOCABULARY AND DEFINITIONS

WHAT FOR PROFESSIONAL ETHICS, EVERYTHING MUST KNOW BABALAWO

1. From memory, a large part of the Ifá literary corpus.
a. Masterfully manipulate the instruments of the oracle of divination.
2. Must be a well-versed interpreter, of the metaphorical language typical of ancestral literature.
3. Know exhaustively, the fauna and flora of your country and the therapeutic and magical utility of a large number of plants.
4. Know the fundamental ideograms (Odù de Ifá) and the incantations inserted in them.
5. You must constantly raise your level of theological and scientific information.

"In Ifá there is not everything, in Ifá everything fits".

This serves as a universal data bank where all existing existential events are stored, classified in the Ifá code.

"The true way to know nothing is to want to learn everything at once"

Ògbè Òdí

SOME ESSENTIAL ELEMENTS FOR THE INTERPRETATION IN THE ACT OF DIVINATION.

Ká firè fún ----- Finish comforting.

A dífá fún ------ He was in search of divination. Lodá fún ------- You will perform the divination.

Mo firè fún ---- Òṣà that we must take as a behavioral reference (her example or behavioral pattern in history or pataki that she refers to).

Abo fún -------- Who is close to the consulted.

Ajogún --------- Bad spiritualities (Death, illness, loss, etc.)

Ayanmó (Añamó) --- Destiny.

Áyewo (Ayeo)   Hex.

Ké fèrí lorí..........Incredulous.

Kán Kán lòní -------- Quickly, today, right now. Kí nnkan má ṣe ---- Protect from evil forces.

Kó le ni ó díwo (Koleniodio) --- It shouldn't be occupying you all the time. Jálè   Complete.

Mo jálè ---- Continue further.

Kòtó jálè --- It is insufficient, follow it or complete it.

é ko yes ---- Begging for something that is not there (is something missing?). Laarí iṣé òrìṣà? ------ Is a job with Ọ̀ṣà important?

Ní torí, Intórí ------- Because of.

Lésè -------- At the foot of, follow the trail. Lówó ------- at the hands of.

Igbó -------- Forest, mone, manigua.

Ode..........Hunter.

Dáfá..........Divination.

SOME IRÉ E IBI (OSOBO) IMPORTANT

IRÉ

Iré aikú -------------------- Health benefit and long life

Iré àṣẹ́ gun ----------------- Benefit to win or conquer

Iré àṣẹ́ gun ọ̀tá ------------ Benefit from defeating enemies

Iré aya -------------------- Profit from a wife

Iré deedeewántòloòkun -Benefit of coming and going to the sea, fishermen, merchants

Iré omaa --------------------Intelligence benefit

Iré ìrìnkiri (inikini) -------- Travel benefit

127

Iré lésè eegún ------------ Benefit at the foot of the dead

Iré lésè ęléda ------------- Benefit at the foot of the creator

Iré mérin layé ------------ Benefit that comes from the four parts of the world

Iré nlǫlé siwaju ------------Benefit of improving by going to another land

Iré nşowó (Iré şowo) ---- Profit of doing business

OSOBO (IBI)

Afitibó --------- Unexpected death

Akóba --------- Unexpected punishment, an unforeseen evil

Àroye...........Complaint

Àrùn (anu).......Disease

Ejo (eyo)..........Judgment

Ikú..............Death

Iyan (iña) ----- Hunger, famine, etc.

Òfo ------------- Irreconcilable loss, divorce, differences

Òràn (ona) ----Big problem

Ònà ----------- leather, bumps

ELEMENTS OF DIVINATION FOR COMMUNICATION WITH ORI (ÌBÒ)

Apadí (Akuadí) ---- Piece of porcelain slab, opposite to iré.

Apa (Akua) --------- Bull's-eye Seed (beat opponents).

Gúngún ------------- (death, deceased and conclude).

Igbin ----------------- Elongated snail (Ayé), means union.

Òtá ------------------ Small stone, longevity and war.

Owó ------------------ Double snail (cowries), currency, profit, acquire. Àwòran (Awona) --Small image of cloth or clay.

Àgbálùmò -----------.Caimito Seed, enjoy life

Efun ----------------- Cascarilla Ball, represents purity.

Eyin (eñi) ---------- Tooth of an animal, irreparable loss.

Isìn ------------------ Seed of the vegetable Cease, represents

Òrúnmìlà. Sáyò ----Guacalote seed, children and multiplicity of goods.

THREE ODÙ MAKE UP A "DETERMINING FIGURE OF IFÁ" WHEN THE ORACLE IS CONSULTED.

Considering that an event is given by a query that a person makes to the Ifá oracle. Three esoteric figures will be considered as a general rule, which from these events emerge to take into account:

The first reading is called: Odù Toyale Iwá (1680 stories; patakí; eses).

This Odù investigates and explains the destiny of the person and in turn represents their problems.

The second reading is called: Odù Okuta Kulá (1680 stories; patakí; eses).

This odù reaffirms in detail what is expressed in the Toyale, it speaks of the causes of the person's problem.

The third spread is called: Odù tomala belanṣe (1680 stories; patakí; eses).

This odù reaffirms what was expressed by the previous ones and in turn provides various possible solutions to the person's problem.

There are also two others important odù to take into account: The Boyuto odù that is a kind of guardian odù of the Toyale odù and its writing results from the opposite writing of its encryption. And the odù Omotorun Iwa which is the odù formed by the union of the ends of the odù Toyale and the odù Tomala belanşe.

Each Odù is supposed to have 1680 of those stories related to him, and this along with those of the other odù, and each one of them is supposed to be known by the Bàbálawo who is the one who guesses and sacrifices, it is expected that he has it in memory, although we have not found any capable of that feat ......

Ifá Divination page 16 Willian Bascom (End of quote).

And we also find that some authors of works and writings specialized in these matters, agree with these criteria.

As each odù will have 1680 possible stories related to it, and with equal possibilities for all. Since the probabilities for the three odù are the same, that is; 256 times for each of the positions in a query to the Ifá oracle, that is: 256x256x256 = $(256)^3$ = 16, 777,216. (Sixteen million seven hundred seventy-seven thouSand two hundred sixteen). This means that there are the same possibilities for each event, if we divide 1 by the number of possibilities in the event, a figure will be so small that it tends to be considered or taken "as zero probability". It is evident that the result of this mathematical operation tells us that it is very unlikely that this same Ifá figure will be repeated for many consecutive events, taking into account that, for a certain figure, there is an intrinsically concatenation of ideas. Expressed and summarized in the odù of Ifá. For these reasons it is practically impossible for any human mind to be able to store, keep in its memory and at the same time process such a volume of information in a minimum of time or duration of a consultation, so that the consultant can be considered optimal conditions and ready, to give an adequate response to each of the issues that you face when consulting the Ifá oracle. Unless, you use modern search and information processing methods that are very fast and efficient. Only Olódùmaré its creator and Òrúnmìlà its interpreter, are able to achieve it efficiently. I suppose that a human being would have to live around 700 years of life, with a brain in optimal conditions to be able to achieve it.

SOME EXPRESSIONS YORÙBÁ

Béè ni.- Yes.

Béè kó / ó ti.- No.

Ẹ̀ṣé.- thanks to you (to a superior or someone older than you).

Óṣe.- thank you (to someone younger than you).

Mo dupé.- I thank you.

To dupe.- We thank you.

Mo dupẹ́ pupò.- I thank you very much.

To dupẹ́ pupò.- We thank you very much.

Kò topic.- You are welcome / It is not mentioned / it is nothing.

Àlàáfíà.- Humbly greeting "be the Good", a way of greeting someone wishing them well at the same time.

Note: This greeting is best used between relatives or with people younger than you. It is not considered an acceptable greeting for an older person. In some cases, this may be the greetings used to greet and show respect to a priest of an Òrìsà, but when used in this way it is accompanied by a specific ritual gesture to distinguish it from a social greeting used between peers.

Ò dàbò.- Goodbye.

Note: This greeting is universally used among peers and is liked by the elderly.

Ẹ má bínú.- I'm sorry (to a superior or someone older than you).

Má bínú.- I am sorry (to a fellow man or someone younger than you).

Ẹ kò topic.- You are welcome / It is not mentioned / is nothing (to a superior or someone older than you).

Kò topic.- You are welcome / It is not mentioned / it is nothing (to a similar or someone younger than you).

¿Kí ni orúkọ rẹ.- What is your name?

Orúkọ mi ni.- My name is.

Note: It is generally considered improper to ask someone's name in Yoruba culture. The idea of introducing yourself greeting, but asking for your name is a concept of cultures foreign to the Yorùbá culture. The exception is when someone older than you ask for your name, this is considered acceptable.

Ẹ dide! - Get up (to a superior or someone older than you).

Ẹ jókòó.- Sit down (to a superior or someone older than you).

Dide! - Get up (to a peer or someone younger than you).

Jókòó.- Sit down (to a peer or someone younger than you).

Ẹ Madide! - Do not stand up (to a superior or someone older than you).

Ẹ má jókòó.- Do not feel (a superior or someone older than you).

134

Madide! - Do not stand up (to a peer or someone younger than you).

Má jókòó.- do not feel (like someone or someone younger than you).

Mo féràn ṛe.- I love him (a person, singular).

Mo féràn yin.- I love you (more than one person, plural).

Mo naa féràn ṛe.- I love him too (one person, singular).

Mo naa féràn yin.- (to more than one person, plural).

VOCABULARY USED

The list in the next section presents some forms commonly used in the Yorùbá language that are directly related to Òrìṣà or to the practice of Ifá.

Abo.- Female (indicates gender, does not speak of a woman).

Abòrìṣà.- A worshiper of the Òrìṣà, most often used in the Diaspora to signify someone who has received some basic initiations. This distinguishes that person from the rest of the community.

135

Àbọrú Àbọyè Àbọṣíṣẹ.- To be able to sacrifice / a prayer for the sacrifice to be heard To be able to sacrifice / a prayer for the sacrifice to be accepted To be able to sacrifice / a prayer for the sacrifice to manifest "Àbọrú, Àbọyè" is considered one of the appropriate greetings for a Babaláwo or Ìyánifá (initiated in Ifá). The priest will return the greeting of "Àbọṣíṣẹ." In many cases and the blessing will extend to the initiate return this greeting. This varies from priest to priest.

Àdìmú.- The food offered to the Ancestors and / or Òrìṣà.

Àdúrà.- Prayer.

Ako.- The male (indicates gender).

Àlàáfíà.- Greeting that means "be the Good", a way of greeting someone and wishing them well-being at the same time. See the important note below the greetings section.

Àṣẹ.- The life force; a common meaning; "The power to manifest" or "is for what".

Awo.- The mystery; a name for all the devotees of Òrìṣà; a name for an individual Òrìṣà priest; a term that identifies the religion of Ifá.

Àyèwò.- Research, often used instead of "Ibi" in divination to indicate the need to investigate the problems further.

136

Baba / Baba my.- Father / my father.

Babalórìṣá.- Male priest of Òrìṣà, often the father of spiritual children.

Cuje.- It is a fine rod made from the branches of the tree ("Rasca Barrigas")

Ẹbọ.- The sacrifice to offer. This can be used to indicate the offering of blood to the Òrìṣà although in the Diaspora this is often used as a term indicative of generally offering something to the Ancestors and the Òrìṣà.

Éérìndínlógún.- The name of the sacred Oracle of the initiates of ìrìṣà.

It also refers to the sixteen cowries used during divination; the translation speaks "twenty minus four" which illustrates the Yorùbá way of calculating certain numbers.

Èèwò.- The taboo.

Ẹgbé.- Society or group of people, for example, Ẹgbé Ọsun is a group of initiates of Ọsun.

Èjè.- Blood.

Ẹmu opé.- The palm wine.

Epo Papua.- Red palm oil.

Ewé.- Leaves or herbs.

Ibi.- Bad luck, bad fortune.

Ìborì.- Ritually serve the head, praising and feeding one's Orí.

Idè.- The ankle bracelet, bracelet or necklace, refers to the sacred articles adorned with Òrìṣà beads, although it is more used in the Diaspora to indicate a bracelet of some kind.

Igbá.- Literally "the gourd", but it is often used to indicate a container filled with the sacred mysteries and the consecrated instruments of the Òrìṣà example, Igbá Ọ̀sun is Ọ̀sun, the sacred ritual container.

Ikin Ifá.- The sacred palm nuts used in the most important divination rituals.

Ilé.- Accommodation, house, describes a family from Òrìṣà.

Ìlèkè.- Literally "the beads" but it is often used to refer to the sacred necklaces adorned with Òrìṣà beads.

I'll go.- Good fortune, good luck.

Ìyá, Ìyá my.- Mother, my mother.

Ìyálórìsà.- Priest woman of Òrìṣà, often the mother of spiritual children.

Obì abata.- The cola nut.

Obìrin.- Female or specifically a woman.

Odù Ifá.- The 256 signs or marks used in Ifá divination that represent the fundamental forces of creation in the universe, it is literally used as a reference to the body of Ifá.

Ògbèrì.- Someone who has not received any kind of initiation into the mysteries of Òrìṣà, a novice.

Ọkùnrin.- The male, specifically a man.

Oloriṣa.- An initiate of the Òrìṣà man or woman. Sometimes this word is used to indicate someone who has been initiated into the mysteries of Òrìṣà but has not been spiritually initiated through the rites of consecration.

Olúwo.- In Ifá this term can be applied to an Ifá priest. The general meaning of the word indicates a person who teaches religion. It may, in some cases, indicate a certain line within the Ifá priesthood.

Omì tútù.- Fresh water

Omìèrò.- Water with consecrated herbs, "tranquilizing water".

Ọmọ.- The child, after spring. This can be used to refer to the biological years of spiritual children.

Ọpèlè.- The Ifá divination chain.

Òrí.- White cocoa butter.

Oríkì.- Name of praise or story; sometimes used as an invocation to the matter of the Oríkì.

Orin.- The song.

Orógbó.- The bitter cola nut.

Ọ̀ṣẹ Dúdú / Ọ̀ṣẹ Aládin.- The black soap.

Ọtí.- A general word for spirits or wine.

Owó.- The money.

Oyin.- Honey.

SOME TERMS

Ajagún - The Yoruba term for warriors like the Orìṣa of protection.

Ajogún - The Yoruba term for denying forces.

Babalawo - The priest with a high degree of knowledge within the religious structure of Ifá.

Eegún - Hereditary entities.

Egúngún - The society within the Yoruba cultural structure that communes with and maintains the traditional directives

140

of the ancestors.

Ehin Iwa - The Yoruba term for after life and reincarnation.

Elegun - Those initiated priests and priestesses who are possessed with the Orișa.

Enìkejì - The Yoruba term for the guardian angel.

Eniyan Gidi - the Yoruba term for the authentic or true human being.

Idé - Sacred beads worn on the left wrist by Ifá devotees.

El llé-Ife - The ancient spiritual capital of the present Yoruba nation.

Ìmoyé - like wisdom

The Fá de Ìpìlé - The process of determining one's African origins, using the Ifá divination system.

Ìrùnmolè - The Yoruba term for divinities.

The Ìyáamí - A Yoruba term for witches (The Mothers).

The chestnut tree - The term applied to the societies of freedom established by the African captives escaped from the "New World". Technically, this word is Spanish and is used for sheep or cattle that have been lost.

Odù - The sacred text and the religious body of Ifá; that was named after the admired wife of Orunmila. Also, the term applied to the vessels containing the consecrated objects of the priests.

Odùdúwà - The patriarch of the current Yoruba nation that he established himself.

Ogbọní - The society of superiors within the present Yoruba cultural context, which maintains the connection with the Earth and the cultural forces of African society.

Olódùmarè - the Creator - God in the Yoruba cultural context.

O'lòrìṣà - The Beginning of the priest or priestess within the Yoruba religious structure.

Òrìṣà - The interpretation of Ifá, of energy forces that emanate from the Creator.

These evolutionary divinities are also declared anthropologically as cultural archetypes of light and avatars.

Òrúnmìlà - The prophet, established by the religious cult of Ifá.

ABOUT THE AUTHOR

Marcelo Madan born in 1944 in Santiago de Cuba. He comes from an Afro-Cuban family with deep religious roots. Consecrated in the orisha Ọbàtàlá since 1951. Awo of Orunmila, consecrated in Ifá as Babalawo by his godfather Ruben Pineda (Baba EjiÒgbè), since 1992. His paternal grandfather, Eligio Madan "Ifanlá" of slave parents brought from Africa and a native of Jovellanos in the province of Matanzas Cuba.

His maternal grandmother María Belén Hernández, a famous Iyalorisha from the city of Havana and consecrated in the orisha Ọbàtàlá. His father Eligio Madan Hernández Awo de Orunmila (Ògbè Owonrin) and consecrated in the orisha Oshun. His maternal grandmother, a famous Iyalorisha from the city of Santiago de Cuba. At the beginning of the forties and fifties Rosa Torrez "Shangó

Gumí", who together with the famous babalorisha also son of Shangó Rinerio Pérez, Amada Sánchez and Aurora La Mar el Oriate Liberato and others, initiate the first settlement of orishas in that city; She is the granddaughter of Ma Braulia, a free woman who came from Africa. Veneranda Constanten, her mother, also consecrated in Obàtàlá (Ewin fún), she dedicated her whole life to religious work together with her mother, Rosa Torrez.

These are the deep ancestral roots of Marcelo Madan, which allowed them, through his consecration from an early age, to acquire the knowledge to carry out his religious literary works. And since then, he has become one of the most important researchers of the "lukumises" religion in Cuba, publishing dozens of books, among which are: the "Treaties of Ifá, Synthesis of the odu of Ifá, Orish Collections, The Oracles of the Orishas, Pocket Manual for Santeros, Meals and Adimú for the Saints among others.

Made in the USA
Thornton, CO
09/27/24 14:38:45

6110f650-d9da-4037-a271-2fd37270f15dR01